$440

MORE THAN 65 INTREPID WRITERS AND TRAVEL EXPERTS REVEAL
FUN PLACES AND NEW HORIZONS TO EXPLORE IN YOUR RETIREMENT

SECRETS
TO AMAZING
RETIREMENT TRAVEL

D1057109

Edited by Mark Evan Chimsky

SELLERS

PUBLISHING

27

To my mother and father.

Published by Sellers Publishing, Inc.

Copyright © 2016 Sellers Publishing, Inc.
All rights reserved.

Sellers Publishing, Inc.
161 John Roberts Road, South Portland, Maine 04106
Visit our Web site: www.sellerspublishing.com • E-mail: rsp@rsvp.com

Design by Faceout Studio

ISBN 13: 978-1-4162-4615-2
Library of Congress Control Number: 2016946079

10 9 8 7 6 5 4 3 2 1

Printed in the United States of America.

Note: *65 Secrets to Amazing Retirement Travel* is an updated edition of the
previously published *65 Things To Do When You Retire: Travel* (2013, Sellers Publishing, Inc.).

Credits: page 399

CONTENTS

Section 1
Travel Prep 101

Section 2
There's Such a Lot of World to See

Section 3
Let's Get Away from It All

Section 4
Voluntourism

Section 5
Family Ties

SECTION 6
Unusual Trips

SECTION 7
Special Places to Live

SECTION 8
Journeys of the Spirit

S E C T I O N 9
Hit the Road, Jack

S E C T I O N 1 0
Sail Away

INTRODUCTION

When you think of traveling, where do you dream of going? Delving into hundreds of Web sites and travel articles, I was amazed by the variety of innovative and fun travel options available to retirees — whether they are looking for physical adventure, or a spiritual journey, or to go sightseeing in far-flung places. The contributors included in 65 *Secrets to Amazing Retirement Travel* cover such fascinating trends as:

- taking a "golden gap year" — Already immensely popular in the U.K., this is a new twist on the common practice of high-school graduates taking a year off to travel before starting college, only this time it's boomers who are taking a year to explore the world before settling into their retirement. In her essay, gap-year expert Jo Carroll explains how you can prepare for your own amazing year of travel.

- going "glamping" — This fusion of glamour and camping is for those travelers who love the outdoors but want to have as many creature comforts as possible when they're communing with nature. Abby Jeffords details the possibilities of how to glamp in style.

- living nomadically — Lynne Martin caused a stir when *The Wall Street Journal* published her lengthy article about how she and her husband sold their home, put their valued possessions in storage, and set off to see the world as "senior gypsies." Her account was immensely popular with *WSJ's* readers, obviously touching a chord with many who dreamed of doing the very same thing. Right after my Publishing Director Robin Haywood showed me the article, I contacted Lynne and she agreed to write a piece on her experiences for this book (by the way, she began her essay in Dublin and finished it while in Marrakech, taking time away from watching snake charmers to complete it!).

- doing "voluntourism" — Why not make the most of your vacation by lending a helping hand in a third-world country or pursuing a passion for archaeology or wildlife while contributing to the efforts of a worthy organization? Ruth Clemmer writes about how she spends her retirement vacations doing archaeological digs, and has already unearthed a portion of a mammoth skull and other bones over 26,000 years old. Another retiree, Warren Stortroen, recounts finding a 3.6 million-year-old fossilized relative of the armadillo, "the size of a small Volkswagen."

This is just a tip of the iceberg of what you'll find in the pages that follow. Hopefully, your imagination will be sparked by the experiences described in the 65 essays in this book. Looking for spiritual rewards? Read Andrew McCarthy's intriguing essay about his pilgrimage to Santiago de Compostela in Spain — and the mysterious man who befriended him along the way. Interested in starting that novel you've always meant to write? Try going to Italy for a women's-only writing workshop led by renowned novelist Elizabeth Berg. Seeking a place with special meaning? Read Sharon Gilchrest O'Neill's moving account of finding her own "Thin Place," a Celtic term for a location where the distance between the physical and the mystical is "thin."

There are many more riches within, waiting to be explored. Which trips and practical tips will resonate with you? Which experiences that you read about will spur you to create your own wonderful adventures? In our lifetime, we go on a number of different kinds of journeys — as you plan your retirement, may this book prove to be a voyage of inspiring discoveries. Safe passage on all your travels . . .

Mark Evan Chimsky

Section

TRAVEL PREP 101

1

Retirement Travel Will Renew Your Sense of Excitement About the World (and Invigorate You at the Same Time)

by Ernie J. Zelinski

Ernie J. Zelinski is an international best-selling author, innovator, professional speaker, and prosperity life coach specializing in creating inspirational books, Web sites, e-books, and seminars that help adventurous souls live prosperous and free. Zelinski is the author of the international best-sellers *The Joy of Not Working* (over 290,000 copies sold) and *How to Retire Happy, Wild, and Free* (over 275,000 copies sold), two life-changing books that have helped hundreds of thousands of individuals around the world achieve a more wholesome life.

Zelinski's books have sold over 925,000 copies worldwide. His recent *Look Ma, Life's Easy (An Inspirational Novel about How Ordinary People Attain Extraordinary Success and Remarkable Prosperity)* teaches people how to actively pursue the alluring rewards of their dreams without compromise or apology.

Zelinski's *Life's Secret Handbook* is a must-have resource for those adventurous souls who need a daily dose of inspiration to follow their dreams and make a big difference in this world.

Zelinski's highly acclaimed philosophy about life reaches over 150,000 individuals a month on his inspirational Web sites and blogs. Meet Zelinski at: www.erniezelinski.com, www.retirement-cafe.com, www.how-to-retire-happy.com, and www.Look-Ma-Lifes-Easy.com.

The retirement life truly worth living is out there in the wooded wilds of the unknown, instead of in the village of certainty and safety. Travel is one of the many ways to experience adventure and the unknown. And, of course, travel is one of the great pleasures of retirement. Travel, however, need not only be done for pure pleasure; it can support one of your purposes or missions in retirement.

Wanting to understand a nation — anything from the people to the history to the economy to the geography to the customs — is an admirable intent indeed. Best of all, your purpose doesn't have to be cast in stone; it can vary from year to year, changing from studying famous works of art to photographing the great sights of the world to experiencing the most inspirational religious sites.

What is the one thing you would enjoy doing on your vacation more than anything else? Then why aren't you working toward making it a reality in your retirement? Below are the top-ten travel goals people selected on a social indexing Web site. You may want to add one or more of these goals to your list of adventures to pursue in your retirement.

- Travel the world.
- See the northern lights.
- Go on a road trip with no predetermined destination.
- Visit all 50 states.
- Backpack through Europe.
- Go on a cruise.
- Go on a road trip.
- Sleep under the stars.
- Visit another country.
- Leave your city once a month. Also, leave your country once a year.

Whatever journey you choose to pursue, travel can enhance your retirement significantly since it provides an elevated degree of stimulation, freshness, and pleasure not encountered in your everyday routine and environment. Of course, travel is a great teacher. Regardless of where you go, you can always learn something new. Learning about the food, the cooking, and the clothing of a country, along with what retirement means to the locals, are just a few things that can broaden your knowledge of the world.

Particularly when you go abroad, travel takes you out of your element and inspires you to new insights about your life in general. It is an effective path to thinking in different ways about the world and what it means to you. Travel to other countries can even jolt you out of your unconsciousness about how good your life is into a deep, conscious appreciation of all the great things that you have going for yourself in retirement.

Perhaps it even makes sense to spend all the money that you can on travel, if that turns you on more than anything else in life. Indeed, you may even want to forget about leaving your children or grandchildren any inheritance and spend the money on as many adventurous treks as you can fit into your retired life. This is exactly what one British couple has in mind.

Adair Skevington, 54, and her husband, Mike, 55, caught the travel bug when they both retired. Five years later, Adair, a former chartered accountant, told an *Observer* newspaper reporter, "It makes us sound awful but, yes, we are happy to spend all the money we have saved over the years on having fun now that we have retired." The Skevingtons, who live in the central-England city of Derby, had just returned from a trip to South Africa and were about to leave on a trip around Europe.

"It really depends on how long we're able to travel, but if we go on like this, we won't be leaving our children anything," declared Adair. "My parents worked until they were 65, by which time they were worn out. If we don't enjoy life now and make the most of it while we're active, we will lose the chance."

If the travel bug gets the best of you in retirement, you may want to stay close to home and discover your own state or region, or you may want to venture to foreign lands. Regardless of how far you go, the degree to which your next trek turns out to be pleasurable, adventurous, and satisfying will depend on how well you plan your trip. The quality of your journey will also depend on your ability to be spontaneous and how well you are able to maintain a positive attitude throughout.

Here are ten tips on how to enhance your next journey:

- Review your passions in life. Incorporate your greatest passion into your vacation plans.

- The key to an enjoyable journey is not to put yourself under stress and duress.
- Try not to schedule too many things to do.
- Have periods of free time that allow for some spontaneity.
- When going on vacation in your car, don't rush to your destination. Take your time. Add to your enjoyment by stopping to read the roadside signs about the historical points of interest.
- If one of your retirement dreams is relocating to another city or country, then head there and treat your vacation as an adventurous research expedition.
- When visiting towns and cities, take the extra time to check out the local cafés and diners instead of eating at the restaurants catering to the tourist trade. You will experience cheaper and better food, as well as a more interesting atmosphere.
- When you have the choice of two exciting things to do, choose the one you haven't tried.
- Get off the beaten path. Don't let your hang-ups interfere with trying new destinations. Journeys that entail learning new things, seeking adventure, meeting interesting people, and experiencing new cultures are the most satisfying.
- Find a pub, coffee bar, or bistro where the locals hang out. Get to know them, along with their

music, their stories, their laughter, and their aspirations.

You may also want to try a working vacation, which is a great way to cut down on the expenses of living in another country. Working holidays, or "volunteer vacations," as they are sometimes called, provide people with an interesting avenue for travel and adventure. Those who have done it feel that taking a working vacation provides a more vigorous and satisfying traveling experience.

Volunteering for overseas assignments can provide many advantages and rewards. These cross-cultural assignments are opportunities to deal with different environments and people. They are also a great way to test your commitment and adaptability while living in a third-world country.

In short, whether it's a journey to all corners of the world or an occasional trek closer to home, travel should be somewhere on your agenda in retirement life. Travel near and far will help you break the routines of everyday life that can lead to staleness and boredom. Above all, regardless of how old you are, travel can renew your sense of excitement about the world and invigorate you at the same time.

2

Travel-Planning Logistics

by Mahara Sinclaire, M.Ed.

Mahara Sinclaire, M.Ed., is the author of *The Laughing Boomer: Retire from Work — Gear Up for Living!* She offers private coaching program called 90 Days to a Life on Fire. Sinclaire and her husband traveled nonstop around the world for nearly three years. She can be reached at www.maharasinclaire.com.

I f travel is one of your top retirement goals, you are not alone! Although it consistently ranks as one of the most important priorities for those who are planning their postwork lives, many only get in one or two trips after they have retired. A big stumbling block is the logistics: *how do you actually make it happen?* Below are some tips.

First, buy a large world map, globe, or atlas. Yes, you can view a map online, but the visual and tactile experience of planning your trip on a wall can't be replicated. Flag your *must-do*, your *like-to-do*, and your *might-do* experiences. Have your travel partner do the same. Indicate several scenarios or routes, or use different colors for two or more people. The anticipation of planning is part of the enjoyment of your trip, but also leave some unplanned routes, because another fun aspect of the travel experience is the serendipitous exploration of new areas. This exercise should lead you to some big-picture conclusions about your general travel plans.

Next, research on the Internet the best times of the year to visit the tentative places you have picked. Notice the geography: the topography and latitude and longitude on the globe. Morocco in July is uncomfortable, and India in February is lovely. Even at the equator, the highest mountains of Ecuador have snow year-round.

After this preliminary research, set a flexible and tentative start date. You might change this date and locations several times as you discover what activities are available during different time frames. As you research the various countries you are considering, pin down the specifics of each country: the highlights, the relative costs, and any danger or concerns that might be present. Get a sense of how much time you might want to spend in one place or region. This is also the time to include your special-interest activities. For example, you may plan your trip to see world tennis tournaments in various countries, or to visit wine regions. We built our trips around art galleries and birding.

Do this research online and with books. Borrow travel guides from the libraries or watch videos on each country. Travel guides are written for specific audiences, so find out which ones reflect the type of travel you want — budget or first class.

The cost of paying for round-the-world tickets can be spread out over one year. The price of global travel can vary considerably, depending on the number of stops and regions you select. Determine the scope of how much you want to see and the time you want to allocate for each leg of your journey. Some people stay only a few weeks in an area and then fly on, while others spend months in a region and explore the surrounding countries by using local transport, such as buses, trains, cruises, and in-country airlines.

At some point in your planning research, you'll want to go online and visit the three major airline alliances, OneWorld, Star Alliance, and SkyTeam. Some sites have interactive features. Although it is possible to purchase your round-the-world tickets online, I recommend you buy them through an insured travel agent. Be aware that it can take time to book these flights.

You already know that large world-class cities in North America, Europe, and Asia are expensive. If that is where you plan to spend much of your time, you will probably need a big budget. Conversely, time in South America, Southeast Asia, and many other countries is much less expensive. Check the World Bank annual income surveys (http://data.worldbank.org/news/2010-GNI-income-classifications) to find the average per capita income for every country in the world. You will find the percentage of total income spent on accommodations and food varies dramatically from country to country. In reality, most people want (or need) to balance time between various countries, so that the total cost of the trip will be less.

Some general points to keep in mind are: going to Europe in the summer is expensive, and any travel plans during major holidays should be booked well in advance. Determine if you want to spend more time exploring culture and bigger cities, or experiencing nature and doing more active traveling. Also, consider cruising through Northern Europe, as the Scandinavian countries are expensive. We found that these cruises offered accommodations, transportation, and food at a daily rate that turned out to be much more economical than if we independently booked our hotels and ate out in restaurants in each port city.

Consider taking "repositioning cruises." These usually occur in the spring and fall, and are called repositioning cruises because the cruise ship is moving from one sailing route to another. For example, ships that ply the Alaska route in the summer move to the Mexican Riviera in the winter, and this trip from the northern West Coast down to Mexico offers exceptional prices. Florida is a repositioning hub for the Caribbean and Europe, specifically the Mediterranean, and there are many one-way cruises available in the spring and fall. Other routes include Vancouver to Beijing, China, and Chile to Florida, both twice yearly. After strenuous traveling, these cruises offer a chance to completely relax.

We've personally booked into two- and three-star

hotels or apartments in different cities and used repositioning cruises as our mode of transportation — and a welcome opportunity for five-star dining.

Once you know where you're going, it's not realistic to plan more than one or two months in advance of your actual trip. That way you can make decisions about staying longer, or moving on. Often safaris or trips such as sailing the Galapagos or exploring the Amazon jungle are better priced in the local currency. You may fall in love with a country, or find it only mildly interesting. You need some plans, but you also need to be able to grab deals when you see them or to move on. We rented apartments in Buenos Aires and Cusco, Peru, for around $1,000 a month, and made our travel plans for the next few months while we were in the area.

One other point is that you will be making your decisions on a variety of things, and price isn't the only criterion. I've observed people paralyzed by trying to get the "best deal." You will pay a bit more sometimes, and other times you'll find some amazing bargains. Or you may strike up friendships with people and be invited to stay in their homes. Keep the big-picture view that in the end it will all be a wash — the most important thing is that you will have had your unique travel experiences. Plan to spend a day or so every couple of months on the Internet looking and booking, but other than that, enjoy the ride. If you're traveling with a partner, share the responsibilities of booking and planning. You will figure out your personal style after a few weeks. There is no single right way.

If you have rented out your house, or otherwise cut your fixed expenses to the bone, you will probably be able to travel around the world for about the same amount of money as staying at home. Also, depending upon your financial situation, spending a bit of your savings that you have worked hard for all your life is worth it. Have fun!

3

Senior Travel Deals: An Overview

by Ed Perkins

Ed Perkins is a nationally known travel writer and consumer advocate. He founded the newsletter *Economy Traveler* in 1976, and he was later named as the first editor of *Consumer Reports Travel Letter*, where he remained for 13 years. Following retirement in 1998, he continues to write two weekly columns syndicated by Tribune Media Service and serves as contributing editor to SmarterTravel.com. He has appeared as a travel expert on a number of national TV programs, is often heard on radio, and has testified before Congress on airline matters. Perkins cosponsored a request to the Federal Trade Commission to clamp down on deceptive hotel-pricing practices. He resides in Ashland, Oregon.

Now that you're a senior, you're expecting lots of terrific travel discounts and deals, right? If so, you're in for a big letdown. Where senior deals could once be really great, travel suppliers have figured out better ways to fine-tune their pricing, and the best senior deals have fallen victim to more sophisticated "yield management" techniques. Still, you do have some options:

Airlines. The once-popular senior coupons and "clubs" are long gone. As of now, the only domestic airline to offer useful senior discounts is Southwest, and even there, the senior deal has limited use. Basically, Southwest routinely offers four fare types. The cheapest by far are the "Wanna Get Away" fares, available to travelers of any age. Though these fares are relatively low, seating is limited, and tickets must be purchased in advance and are nonrefundable. There are senior fares available (but not as low as the "Wanna Get Away" rates); the advantage is that this fare is available up to the last minute, it's fully refundable, and it's a better rate than similar tickets for other travelers. However, seniors who can qualify for a restricted any-age ticket will end up paying a lot less. Many other airlines say that they still offer senior discounts, but over the last decade, I haven't found any, nor have I seen any overseas. *Conclusion:* Except for Southwest, forget senior airline discounts and get the best any-age deal you can find.

Hotels. Most hotels — especially the budget chains —

routinely offer discounts of 10 percent to 15 percent to "senior" travelers. Some require AARP membership (age 50 or over), some don't. But these senior deals are generally the same as discounts to members of AAA and other large groups. More expensive hotels may give similar discounts, although they may also offer discounted nonrefundable advance-purchase senior rates. I haven't seen senior hotel discounts anywhere in Europe or Asia. *Conclusion*: Consider a senior hotel discount as a fallback position if you can't score a better deal available to travelers of any age.

Rail. Amtrak offers 15 percent discounts to seniors age 65 or over on most coach-class travel, but not for business class or sleepers. VIA Rail Canada offers variable discounts, usually 10 percent, on coach-class travel to seniors age 60 or over, but it offers much better last-minute discounts to travelers of any age. Discounted BritRail Passes and single-area rail passes for France, Italy, and the "Balkans" are available to seniors age 60 or over, and several countries, including France, Italy, and the U.K., sell senior ID cards that provide 25–50 percent discounts on individual tickets for a full year. Buy rail passes *before* you leave North America, and buy the senior ID cards *after* you arrive abroad. I haven't seen senior rail discounts anywhere else. *Conclusion*: If you qualify, in general you aren't likely to do any better than the senior deal for rail travel in the U.S. and some European countries, but in Canada, special promotions can be a lot better.

Cruises. The big mass-market cruise lines sometimes offer modest discounts to seniors, at varying ages, including some through AARP, but pricing is variable and chaotic. *Conclusion*: The only way you can tell if a senior cruise deal is good is to check the alternative deals for travelers of any age.

Rental cars. Big rental-car companies give senior discounts of usually no more than 10 percent on weekly rentals to members of AARP, and sometimes more on inflated daily rates. They generally give similar discounts to any-age members of AAA and major travel clubs. Although other programs often match this rate, AARP rentals from the giant multinationals have the benefit of significantly superior liability-insurance coverage. Some countries overseas impose a maximum-age cutoff, including Israel (age 75) and Romania (age 70), although individual agencies in other countries may have age limits as well. *Conclusion*:

Unless you can find a better deal, use AARP for the insurance benefit.

Package tours. Tour operators typically don't have enough margin to discount their prices, but many of them target senior travelers with a combination of senior-themed programs and adult education. The biggest by far is Elderhostel, but others include Eldertreks, Great Circle Tours, Grandtravel, and Senior Women's Travel. AARP also offers some senior tour deals. *Conclusion*: Don't look for preferential pricing; look for the tour you want.

Public transit. Transit systems in many big U.S. cities offer senior rates, typically starting at age 65. The best deals are in Pennsylvania, where a Medicare card gets you on Philadelphia and Pittsburgh city transit for free, and on Philadelphia suburban rail for $1 a ride. Many cities offer discounts of up to 50 percent on one-trip fares, multiday passes, or both; many include suburban as well as urban transit. Some cities require you to obtain a senior ID in order to qualify, and increasing numbers of cities, including Boston and Chicago, limit senior transit IDs to local residents. Cities outside the U.S. tend not to offer senior discounts. *Conclusion*: Any time you plan to visit a big U.S. city, check with its transit system for possible senior deals.

Pairing up. Seniors who are single will find that hotel, cruise, and tour pricing is almost always geared to couples. Single travelers have three options: travel alone and pay a "single supplement," which may be almost double but is sometimes much less; sign up for a cruise or tour that offers dedicated single-occupancy rooms or cabins; or find another single to share double-occupancy accommodations. If you can't enlist a friend or relative to share, some cruise lines and tour operators charge you half the double rate and match you with another single of the same sex, or you can sign up for outfits such as Singles Travel International that will help you find and meet possible companions before you book your trip.

AARP. Overall, AARP provides very few discounts that aren't duplicated through other sources. But it does combine, in one place, a long list of senior deals that are often as good as — and sometimes better than — senior deals you can find anywhere else. *Conclusion:* Membership in AARP is worth the annual fee, but before you take an AARP discount, always check for a better any-age option.

4

Rewire® Your Travel

by Jeri Sedlar and Rick Miners

Jeri Sedlar and Rick Miners, a husband-and-wife consulting
team, are coauthors of *Don't Retire, REWIRE!*® 5 *Steps to Fulfilling
Work That Fuels Your Passion, Suits Your Personality, and Fills Your
Pocket.* They are the creators of the concept of rewiring® and
rewirement.® Sedlar is an internationally recognized speaker
and served as the senior advisor at the Conference Board
on the Mature Workforce. Miners was cofounder of FlexCorp
Systems, a business process outsourcing company that had
1,000 employees, including 300 retirees who came back to
work. He sold his company in 2006. They travel the globe
speaking and consulting on transition and personal growth.
Their Web site is www.dontretirerewire.com.

When we began doing research for our book
Don't Retire, REWIRE!® we asked people
why they work beyond a paycheck. To our
amazement, individuals reported 85 different reasons,
including: to have accomplishments, to be part of
the action, to be creative, to have structure, to be
connected to others, to develop skills and talents, etc.

We call these reasons "drivers"; that is, the emotional dividends we get from doing something that stimulates, nourishes, and sustains us in the most positive ways. We get driver fulfillment in a variety of ways: at work, at play, or participating in leisure activities, like traveling or going on a vacation, which can be a source of huge satisfaction. Some of the benefits derived from traveling can be continuous learning, encountering new experiences, becoming an authority on a subject, having fun, gaining awareness of global opportunities, pursuing a passion, and making a difference — for example, you can do volunteer travel that involves working on a project to better the lives of others, e.g., digging a well in India, working at an orphanage in Africa, building environmental-friendly trails in the Andes, etc.

It is not surprising that when we ask our readers and audiences to discuss their plans for the future, the subject of travel is usually high on their bucket list. A trip or vacation is a great reward for long hours spent working, meeting deadlines, enduring long commutes, dealing with demanding bosses, clients, or customers, and handling the stress of a 24/7 world. It is a great way to start a transition to the next phase of your life. Developing a bucket list of numerous destinations is the best way to begin. The longer it is, the better it is. Don't just think next year. Think the next 20 years. Write down where you want to go and what you want to do. You will find that by making such a list, you will start to get very enthusiastic about the possibilities and the opportunities that the future holds.

Remember that a retirement travel list should be created using this motto: Do *the heavy lifting first*. By heavy lifting, we mean taking the trips that are the longest or the most physically taxing in the early years of retirement, when your stamina and strength are at a higher level. Climbing Mount Kilimanjaro, walking the Great Wall of China, or going up and down steep steps at a temple ruin is a lot more enjoyable when your body is up to the challenge. This way, you won't miss out on places because you waited too long. Reserve cruising or more sedentary vacations for when you are past the age for arduous travel.

Unfortunately, when we ask people where they are planning on traveling to in the future, we often hear the response, "I don't know. I guess I will go wherever my wife (or husband) wants to go." They admit that they have never really had the time to think of travel.

They were too involved with work or taking care of their parents or children. We remind them to let the kite out and imagine where they have always wanted to go.

Travel requires planning and budgeting . . . a little or a lot . . . depending on where you want to go and what you want to do. There can be big trips and little trips, or vacations sitting on a beach, or visits to distant family and friends. Some wonderful travels can be done on a low budget. Using your imagination and creativity and doing the planning yourself can lead to roads less traveled and exciting destinations that are relatively tourist free.

Traveling can be active or passive. You can go and just see things, or you can be an active participant. As one of our readers said, "I had the choice of taking a cruise and sitting in a deck chair, or going sailing with a group of friends. I chose sailing with friends. I got to hoist the sails and navigate." Another said, "I wanted to tour the vineyards of Burgundy. I had a choice of driving a car or pedaling a bike. I chose a bike." Others reported that all they wanted to do was to show up and have everything done for them. As the saying goes, "Whatever floats your boat."

You can go it alone, or travel with friends or with a group of people you've never met before. Many feel safer in a crowd, particularly if they are going to a destination far from home. What a wonderful experience it can be to go with others with whom you share common interests and curiosity about a location or activity. You learn together from the guides and each other. Those who like to travel independently — as an individual or as a couple — enjoy the freedom to stop where and when they choose, avoiding the regimens and distractions of a group.

Couples who disagree on where to go might consider taking separate trips. Going alone or with a friend doesn't mean "I don't love you." It means that you each get to see what you want and return with new stories about what you have seen. There is nothing wrong with that.

Two thousand years ago, the Roman philosopher Seneca captured what's best about travel: "Travel and change of place impart new vigor to the mind." We call it *Rewired*® *Travel*. It rewires, stimulates, excites, and surprises. Now, go and start planning that trip of a lifetime!

5

The Art of Authentic Travel

by Doris Gallan

Doris Gallan is the author of *The Boomers' Guide to Going Abroad to Travel | Live | Give | Learn*. She has traveled around the world twice, journeying to all seven continents, visiting over 50 countries, and living in six. Gallan is a consultant to the travel and tourism industry, providing advice on creating and marketing products to her fellow baby boomers. She can be reached through her Web site: www.BabyBoomersTraveling.com.

I've met hundreds of experienced travelers who excitedly talk about their fantastic journeys where they "really connected" with the people, the culture, and the place. I used to get a little jealous when they shared their stories about the amazing meals they had with people from around the world, and the wonderful music and dancing they enjoyed at festivals they just happen to have discovered in their travels. The icing on the cake was when they'd show me fabulous photos of places that tourists usually never get to see.

I used to wonder: "How come some people can practically count on having such terrific experiences traveling, while others never seem to even come close?"

I decided to find out for myself and to put into practice whatever it took to have amazing vacations. This is what I learned: all it takes is time, finding the right place, guts, and making an effort.

Making Every Trip an Authentic Cultural Experience

I've learned that there are plenty of opportunities for us to have great travel adventures — we just don't always know they exist. To take advantage of them, we need to be receptive to the possibilities, recognize them when they occur, and take steps to enjoy them before it's too late.

Of course, that's all easier said than done when I'm struggling with the language, the food, the maps, and a million other details of traveling in a foreign country. But here's what I do to open myself up to authentic cultural experiences:

Time. When I plan my trips, I schedule more time in fewer places so that I can get a feel for the locals and, hopefully, connect with some of them. The more often they see my smiling face, the more likely they'll smile back and maybe strike up a conversation. This happens when I return to the same restaurants a few times, or shop in the little grocery stores close to where I'm staying, or even just walk along the neighborhood streets.

Place. A great place to meet local people is through the owners of small hotels. That's why I often book a room at a charming inn rather than at a big chain. The managers of these smaller places are invariably more available — and approachable — than those at big hotels. Also, most innkeepers will freely share their advice about where to eat, sightsee, and swim, and they'll even give you a few pointers on where to get the best deals on souvenirs.

Guts. No guts — no authentic travel. I could make this my motto and have it tattooed on my arm. My best travel experiences have come from taking risks. They were small risks, mind you, but a lot of travelers won't even go so far as to talk to strangers on trains, buses, and planes, or on the street, or in restaurants. Even when I don't speak the local lingo, I use a combination of a language "cheat sheet" and pantomime.

It's not easy putting yourself out there this way, and

that's a big reason why many people don't experience authentic travel. They're hesitant to connect with residents of a city or town. But I've found that when I open myself up to ridicule and laugh at myself when I goof up, I show people that I trust them. And they, in turn, trust me. And that's the start of connecting.

Effort. It may take more effort to make all the arrangements myself or to slip away from a tour group for a day to go to a nontourist market on my own, but that's when I have the best travel adventures. Any time a large group arrives at a destination, it changes the dynamics of the place. If you want to get a feel for what a place is really like, you sometimes have to move away from the pack and do a bit of exploring on your own.

Authentic Travel Through Tour and Cruise Companies
I'm often told that it's impossible to have authentic travel experiences through organized expeditions. Travelers tell me that they have felt rushed on some tours and cruises as they are herded from one crowded tourist destination to another.

I agree that this may be true for some. But I've had a number of wonderful experiences on both tours and cruises, especially when I use smaller companies that are more responsive to the individual needs of baby boomers who are seeking a genuine and meaningful vacation. When I book a tour or cruise, I look for a company that:

- allows several days to a week in one location and permits enough free time for me to wander on my own.

- takes travelers to places other than standard, overdeveloped tourist destinations. For example, on one tour I was on, we brought school supplies to an African village school. On another vacation, I took an Antarctic cruise and learned a lot from the educational programs that were held on the ship, featuring seminars with four scientists.

- introduces me to the residents of a city or town, not just those working in the tourism industry. My favorite was a home stay with a family in the Amazon forest of Brazil. It gave my husband and me a chance to connect with local people, while providing a bit of income for our hosts.

It's not always easy to find companies that provide what I look for in tours and cruises. I've found that smaller companies focusing on specific interests are better able to give me the authentic travel experience I seek. Specialty tours and cruises can more easily arrange visits to the kind of villages and ports that are more likely to have retained a greater degree of their culture.

The more time you spend in one place — whether on a tour, a cruise, or traveling independently — the more comfortable you'll become with the language, the currency, the layout of the area, and how the transportation system works. You'll also start talking to residents who may suggest places to see and things to do.

I'm like millions of other boomers who won't go home satisfied until they've had the opportunity to learn something new and connect with the locals. That means it's worth the extra effort to pick up a bit of the language, to chat with strangers, to find tours and cruises that meet my needs, and to put myself out there so that residents see enough of me to want to start talking with me.

It's this human exchange between two cultures that transforms tourists into travelers. That, to me, is the joy of authentic travel.

6

Solo Travel: A Great Way to Enjoy Newfound Freedom

by Janice Waugh

Janice Waugh is the author of *The Solo Traveler's Handbook*; the publisher of Solo Traveler (www.solotravelerblog.com), the blog for those who travel alone; and the moderator of the Solo Travel Society on Facebook (http://facebook.com/solotravelsociety/), with over 198,000 likes. She has spoken at the Smithsonian on solo travel and at a number of industry events. She has been quoted in many media outlets, including CNN, *The Washington Post*, the *Chicago Tribune*, the LA *Times*, and USA *Today*. Waugh lives in Toronto, Canada, and has a master's degree in History.

"Freedom and personal autonomy are more important to people's well-being than money. . . ."
—American Psychological Association

Yes, the adage is true: money can't buy happiness. In fact, the findings of a number of studies show that choice and autonomy are greater predictors of happiness than money. If autonomy and choice are fundamental to happiness, then taking a break from others and learning to live on your own terms is important. Whether you're single or have a partner, solo travel is your opportunity to do this, offering you the chance to . . .

- feel absolutely free.
- gain confidence by being independent.
- discover who you are when you're not meeting the demands of others.
- spend time developing your talents or discovering new ones.
- build new self-esteem, now that work is not part of your identity.
- return home happy.

Happiness can be elusive. The number of self-help books on the subject confirms this. Maybe we all need a little time to ourselves, to make decisions, discover our strengths, and experience more autonomy. Maybe we all need to travel solo.

The Joy of Solo Travel for All

It doesn't matter whether you're single or in a relationship — solo travel is an enriching experience. Traveling solo allows you to explore on your own schedule. It lets you go where you want, when you want, without being dragged places by others or feeling that you are dragging someone else. In addition, because you are alone, you will meet other travelers and locals more easily. Rather than being focused on a companion, you are open to what and whom is around you. This results in many wonderful chance encounters and often lifelong friends.

There are as many ways to travel solo as there are people. Some return to their backpacking days of the 1960s and roam by train or bus from hostel to hostel. Yes, hostels are no longer exclusively for young people. As boomers have aged, hostels have changed, and now many offer private rooms. You will find more younger people than older in a hostel, but many retirees as well. It's a great way to act and feel youthful.

At the other end of the spectrum are tours, resorts, and cruises that take care of all the travel details for you. I particularly recommend river cruises, which are like moving hotels, and which stop daily so that travelers can experience cities, large and small, along the way. They leave plenty of free time for you to explore and, unlike ocean cruises, day tours are often included in the price.

Solo Travel Is a Safe Choice

Many people who have not traveled solo wonder whether it is safe. Most places are, especially if you have reached retirement age. You have the life experience that tells you how to avoid potential problems and, if you should find yourself in a difficult situation, you'll have the know-how to get out of it quickly.

Since I've written extensively on safety, I'd like to share the following basic rules that I think are worth highlighting:

Stay in public. This is my number-one rule: I stay in busy, public places. Regardless of how comfortable I am with new acquaintances, I rarely leave a public place with them. And I strategize to avoid this, so that I don't insult them with my caution. For example, I will discreetly call a cab before anyone can offer me a ride.

Be proactive in choosing whom to connect with. Because I take the first step in choosing whom to speak with — and I'm discerning about this decision — I believe that it's unlikely that I'll connect with someone who's inappropriate.

Engage other people in your safety. If I'm walking to a destination but I'm no longer sure of my safety, I'll stop and ask directions even if I know the way. People will redirect me if I'm headed into an unsafe area. When I go out at night, I connect with the bartender or a server, so that they are aware that I'm alone. They'll watch out for me and move unwanted attention away. Whenever possible, I subtly engage others in my safety.

Never be rushed into a decision. This is the easiest way to be conned or ripped off. It's a common strategy of people who want to take you for more than they should. So, if you feel rushed, slow things down or move on. This can happen in a regular transaction at a market or when someone on the street looks like he's raising funds for a good cause but has other motives in play.

Be rude if necessary. I'm usually courteous and congenial with everyone I meet. It makes for a happier life. However, when it comes to safety, if being polite doesn't work I allow myself to be rude — especially when I travel solo. If someone is bothering you, raise your voice if necessary. The mere fact that you will do this will usually send the offending person away.

Follow these principles and such basic precautions as carrying identification, having the name and phone number of your hotel in your pocket, and keeping your passport and money secure, and you should be safe when you travel solo.

Go Out and Enjoy a Great Solo Travel Experience
Age is a curious thing. When young, you're never old enough. Just a few years later, you can feel too old — a joke to anyone who's a decade or more older than you are. It's important to celebrate your age, no matter what it is. Know that you are enriched by your years, and be grateful for the experience that allows you to see the world in ways that would not otherwise be possible.

When you travel solo, do so within your comfort zone and, maybe, just a little beyond. Enjoy the freedom, confidence, and happiness you'll feel.

7

Is Traveling Really the Retirement Dream?

by Jim Yih

Jim Yih is a financial expert. Visit his award-winning blog, RetireHappyBlog.ca.

When it comes to retirement planning, it is just as important (if not more so) to think about and to plan your postwork lifestyle as it is to plan financially. After all, how would you know how much money you need if you had no idea what you were going to do with your time?

Planning Your Lifestyle

In our retirement workshops, we encourage participants to think about what they want to do when they retire, because the last thing anyone wants in retirement is to become bored.

So, in order to have a fulfilling retirement, you'll want to keep busy doing the things you love. It's about choice and the freedom to do *what* you want, *when* you want, and *how* you want. It's essential to define these goals in detail and to think about some of the activities you want to do when you retire.

What Do You Want to Do When You Retire?

Ask people what they want to do when they retire, and the most common response is "travel." In fact, in every single workshop, when we ask this very question at least 50 percent of participants write down something to do with travel.

Now, I am all for traveling in retirement. In fact, I love traveling myself. It's easy to understand why most people want to travel more in retirement. That being said, I think that this is most people's number-one response because of something I call "retirement pornography."

What Is Retirement Pornography?

If a company is advertising something to do with retirement, what pictures and images does it typically use? Palm trees, beaches, blue sky, cold drinks, oceans, swimming pools, golf courses, and older people with gray hair and really sexy bodies in bikinis and Speedos.

As a result, if you haven't really thought much about what you plan to do when you retire, traveling becomes the easy, automatic answer. It's a sexy answer, the one that society has put in your head as something you are supposed to do when you retire in order to have a successful life after work. But does retirement really look like this?

How Much Traveling Are You Really Going to Do?

For most people, traveling is an activity you do some of the time, but rarely is it something you do *most* of the time.

It's pretty rare for retirees to travel 365 days of the year. It's even unusual to see retirees that travel for half the year. Some (like snowbirds) do head to warmer climates for part of every year, but often, they're just setting up a second home base for half the year, and this is much different than the pulling-a-suitcase-through-airports kind of travel.

In most cases, traveling in retirement is the same as traveling before retirement. It's what you do when you aren't busy with whatever you do for most of your time. Before retirement, that was work — but what about in retirement? If all of your retirement plans center around the three to four weeks you are going to travel, then what are you going to do for the other 48 weeks of the year? We teach people that planning for retirement is about more than just your travel plans. It's about planning your life at home.

Home Is Where the Heart Is

When I use the word "home," I'm not referring to your physical household, but rather to your everyday life. Plenty of people are living incredibly successful, purposeful, and meaningful lives in retirement, doing very ordinary things.

After all, even the most passionate world travelers love the feeling of coming home — to their own routines, their friends, their family, and their own bed.

I believe that the way to have a successful retirement is to think about life *beyond* globe-trotting and to understand what it is you really want to do when you come back home.

Improve Your Retirement Travel with Internet Tools and Social Media

by Ron Mercier

Ron Mercier is retired from his corporate career and currently blogs on topics such as building social networks and planning activities targeted for the 50+ population of baby boomers and retirees.

Traveling is a popular activity for retirees to have on their bucket list. More and more retirees are making extensive use of the Internet and social media for planning trips and related activities, but they can also benefit from these powerful tools during their vacation to get the most out of every journey. While they're away, they can remain in touch with friends and family; by keeping connected, they can even feel more peace of mind staying on vacation for a longer period of time.

Travel Is One of the Best Retirement Activities

Whether you go traveling as a freestyle adventurer or as a member of a tour group is dependent on your personality, your sense of independence, and your confidence level. There are times when traveling in a tour group is the only way to experience a country and understand its history. If you are not comfortable traveling alone, taking a guided tour is an excellent way to experience a new city, and it provides opportunities to meet and get to know fellow travelers as well.

I happen to like traveling, and my preference is to explore without a tour whenever possible. I'm sure that this is in part because most of my professional career involved a lot of business travel, where I had to discover new places on my own. My advice to retirees who'd like to be freestyle travelers is to learn to strike out on your own and to interact with new people. I see many baby boomers traveling in groups of four to eight people; they tend to stick together instead of reaching out to fellow travelers or locals. Meeting and exchanging conversations with people you don't know, especially local citizens, will enhance your understanding of their customs and will likely lead to the creation of new and lasting friendships.

Take More Time to See the World

One of the benefits of traveling after retirement versus taking a vacation from work is that you don't necessarily need to restrict the length of time of your stay. Using Internet tools, you can remotely support your personal affairs using online banking and bill payments. Make use of your ability to stay longer than the average week or two to get better deals on lodging. Increasing the length of your vacation also helps you become more familiar with the culture and people, something you couldn't do while you were employed.

In my travels, whether domestic or international, I notice that many retirees are traveling in greater numbers as freestyle adventurers. Successful travelers make extensive use of the Internet and social media sites to plan their trips from home. Collaborative social-media sites like TripAdvisers and VRBO® (Vacation Rentals By Owners) obtain valuable feedback from patrons about an establishment. I like perusing these sites before going on a trip, to gather information from a variety of individuals. There was a time when the only reviews were from disgruntled travelers who would leave negative comments, but more and more people are voluntarily providing balanced and helpful reviews, without having an "axe to grind." Look closely for trends in these reviews; for instance, if a lot of different people are saying the same thing about a hotel's accommodations, then such a critical mass of opinion should carry weight when you make a decision about whether or not to book a room there.

Put the power of the Internet to use when you're on vacation. The Internet is widely available, regardless of where you travel, and devices like tablets and smartphones allow for effective usage of this technology. By and large, many establishments offer free Internet access and Wi-Fi links to patrons, so the cost is minimal in most instances. Ten years ago, I traveled extensively in Australia and carried my 12-pound laptop to Internet bars, paying connection charges ranging from $8 to $12 per connection. Many times, I would be at locations with little to no Wi-Fi connection, since its use was not as prevalent as it is today. I still travel with a laptop, because of my need for a larger keyboard and a few applications I rely on for managing my business. But my smartphone has all the functions to communicate, and its size and weight are significantly more desirable for travel.

Using a tablet or a smartphone is actually all that one needs to keep in touch during most trips. Be wary, however, of using the cell phone connection while away from your hometown; roaming charges can be quite high, especially in international destinations. I like to disable my cell phone option and just use Wi-Fi on these devices.

Overall, this has become the best era to travel, because our ability to network and communicate has never been so sophisticated — and so user-friendly. As you contemplate your next trip, think about how you can utilize technology to make your vacation as fun as possible. Being able to stay in touch with loved ones may be just the ticket — whether you're on the go in London, Paris, or Rome, or lounging on a tropical beach.

9

Leveraging Excess Good Credit

by Rick Ingersoll

Rick Ingersoll is the foremost expert on frugal travel and flying for free. Every day he teaches his readers how to see the world for pennies on the dollar. You can read about his adventures and his techniques at www.FrugalTravelGuy.com.

Before I retired to travel the world, I was a mortgage-banking-business company owner, loan underwriter, and servicer. In those 12 years, I got to see thousands of different credit reports — the good and the awful. I've also spent time counseling veterans at a local VA office, helping them get out of financial jams and restore their credit scores. I've seen it all, and I'd like to provide you with valuable tips that can help you afford to go on some dream vacations in your retirement years.

Let's start with a few basic pointers on credit. Most people only investigate what kind of credit score they have when they absolutely need to: when they are applying for a loan from a bank, need a mortgage, or want a credit card. These lending institutions set a primary benchmark — a minimum credit score — to determine an applicant's eligibility for approval. All other factors being equal, it takes a certain score in order to be approved for that loan.

For example, if a mortgage lender sets its benchmark for a home loan at a 720 FICO credit score, all those applicants with scores above that magic number will be approved. What if your credit score is 760? You'll be approved, in the same way that an applicant with a credit score of 795 would be. Do you receive a better deal on a home loan if your score is 760? Nope. You just have an excess of good credit — 40 points worth.

And there's a lot you can do with that credit.

In late 2009, credit-card issuers drastically increased the sign-up bonuses offered to new credit-card applicants. Bonuses of 50,000, 75,000, and even 100,000 frequent- flyer miles swiftly replaced meager 25,000-mile bonuses and became the new norm. Typically, these miles are worth about two cents each, so you can see why the excitement — and the number of new applications — skyrocketed.

Many of these benefits are automatically credited to your account after you make your first purchase on the new card. If you have a good credit score, you can judiciously apply for numerous premium travel cards and collect bonuses from each card. The points and miles can really start to add up fast.

But first things first: you need to know your credit score.

If it's been a while since you've checked what your credit score is, CreditSesame.com and CreditKarma.com are both great and easy places to get started. Each site quickly checks with one of the credit-reporting bureaus (CreditSesame uses Experian, and CreditKarma uses TransUnion). They perform a "soft credit check," which means that there will be no impact to your credit score for accessing the information.

Once you are armed with your credit score, it's time to put that excess good credit to work for you.

Credit-card issuers often look for a credit score above

700 on a FICO scale or above 800 on a VantageScore scale. If your credit score is below these numbers, you don't have excess good credit to work with. Get your scores up before applying for any premium travel cards, to ensure that each application generates an approval. And take note of the fact that each credit-card application will lower your credit score between two and five points, so you'll want to make sure you have enough extra good credit built up to absorb this without any negative impact.

A lot of people are afraid to sign up for credit cards. They're afraid of the way it may affect their credit report, or they're afraid of the interest rates. The two-to five-point hit you'll take on your credit score per application falls off your credit report after two years, and in the meantime, the increase in your available credit will actually boost your credit score after a while. As for interest rates, I always recommend that you pay off your entire credit-card bill every month, so you won't have any interest rates to worry about. Making interest payments is the same thing as giving money back to your credit-card company. It negates those rewards that you're getting.

This technique is not for everyone, but I can help you navigate the sometimes intimidating world of credit, credit cards, and bonus points. Once you feel comfortable enough, apply for your first batch and see for yourself how rewarding an experience this can be!

My personal credit file is far from small. I have over 95 entries in it, and my credit score is still excellent. Last year, my wife and I received over one million airline miles and hotel-rewards points just by applying for new premium-travel credit cards and taking advantage of the initial sign-up bonuses being offered. I wasn't kidding when I said that it all adds up! We have been using this technique for the last three years, and in that time we have visited over 64 countries, covering each trip with bonus miles and points.

One of the easiest ways to understand how this all works is through an example:

Someone I work with named Katie wanted to fly abroad to meet her boyfriend in London; she was looking for a round-trip flight plus four nights in a hotel. Katie had a 725 FICO credit score and usually had expenditures of $2,000 per month that she put on her credit cards. She was diligent about paying off this amount in full each month, to avoid racking up high interest charges. Typically, her trip to London would cost around $2,500. But I helped her choose the right credit cards to get the flight and the hotel — *for under $200 in fees.*

The first thing to figure out is how to get there. There are a number of credit cards that will help you fly to London. One of my favorites is the US Airways Chairman's Preferred Dividend Miles Premier World MasterCard. At this point in time, the card gives you a large amount of bonus miles with its first use, enough in fact to get a round-trip ticket from the United States to London during off-peak season on US Airways. Plus, there's no annual fee. So, for just spending two dollars at Starbucks, you can get a trip to London!

Next to figure out: the hotels. It's hard to get four nights in a single hotel with only one credit-card bonus. It is, however, possible to get four nights at different hotels using two different cards. And that's what Katie did. She signed up for two hotel-affiliated credit cards, and earned free nights at both hotels as part of their promotions — for one card, she needed to spend $1,000 in the first three months to earn two free nights; for the other card, she needed to spend $2,500 in four months to earn two free weekend nights. So, for under $200 in combined fees for the hotel-affiliated credit cards (and by putting $3,500 on her credit cards, which she was going to spend anyway), Katie got four nights in hotels in London. Two hotel-affiliate cards I highly recommend are the Chase® Hyatt Credit Card and the Citi® Hilton HHonors™ Reserve card.

It all takes a bit of planning and some decent math and organizational skills, but when you use your excess credit, the whole world can open up to you. From Machu Picchu to the Cape of Good Hope, from the Pyramids to the Eiffel Tower, you can see it all. Trust me, I have.

10

Shopping Across Borders for Medical Care

by Ilene Little

Ilene Little is the CEO of Traveling 4 Health & Retirement (THR). She started this consumer-reporting Web site to facilitate unfiltered conversations between consumers and international medical and lifestyle professionals, as well as with people who travel overseas for treatment or to manage their health-care needs. Little has the exclusive medical-tourism blog on www.escapeartist.com. In addition, she hosts the "Know Before You Go" show, broadcast weekly on www.overseasradio.libsyn.com. She's also on the Web sites of several physicians and medical researchers, and is quoted in *Saving Private Healthcare* by Michael Kalthoff. Her own book is *How to Plan a Successful Medical Tourism Trip*.

You can't control the changes in the health-care industry, but you can implement your own health-care strategy and, therefore, improve your quality of life. Attitude, knowledge of your own health risks, and insisting on the best medical care are all within your control.

When Choosing an Overseas Hospital

If you are considering traveling overseas for a medical procedure, there are resources available to help you. Traveling 4 Health & Retirement (THR) advocates seeking a high standard of satisfaction from treatment abroad. This consists of the following factors:

Clinical Experience

- Was the patient provided a written care plan?
- Did the treatment accomplish the stated goal(s) of the care plan?
- Were there any complications?
- If there were complications, why, and how were they managed?

Customer Experience

- Was the patient provided with a written cost of treatment?
- Was the estimate accurate within 15 percent of the final bill?
- If the final bill was greater than 15 percent of the estimate, was the variance explained by the doctor and the hospital?
- Did the hospital staff speak your language?
- Was the staff helpful?
- Would you rate your overall experience as favorable?

Mitigating the Risk of Surgery Abroad

Traveling 4 Health & Retirement recommends that patients strongly consider booking their medical procedure through a professional T.P.A. (Third-Party Administrator) that offers professional medical case-management services that adhere to American standards of case management and medical planning.

It makes sense to research medical travel by reaching out to the medical-travel experts. At THR, we offer consumer-protection tools that provide peace of mind, including:

1) step-by-step and one-on-one consultation and guidance for the "do it yourself" medical traveler

2) referrals to patient advocates trusted by THR members, and

3) an American health-care executive providing financial- and medical-oversight case management.

Whether you decide to travel or live overseas (full- or part-time) for medical reasons, you'll want to educate yourself on all the resources available to you. No advice is more reassuring than the firsthand experiences of your friends who live part-time or full-time abroad. Start making those new friends.

Traveling Sin

by Rick Kimball

Richard S. (Rick) Kimball is a Maine-based freelance writer and photographer. He and his wife, Tirrell, own and operate Green Timber Publications, a small press producing religious education curricula for use in Unitarian Universalist congregations. Kimball began his writing and editing career as a reporter, columnist, and city editor at what was then the Guy Gannett newspapers of Portland, Maine. He next became a full-time writer and editor for J. Weston Walch, Publisher, producing supplementary educational materials for secondary schools. He has written religious education material for the national Unitarian Universalist Association, and in the areas of creativity, local history, and human sexuality. He holds a bachelor's degree from Harvard College, and a master's from Columbia University Graduate School of Journalism.

When I was a teen, my friends and I would sometimes grill each other after dates. "How far did you get?" we would ask with a leer. We did not expect or perhaps want a true answer. We were not even sure how far any of us really wished to get. We only knew we were supposed to try and "go all the way" — to commit an act that some called sin.

Sin was different on the basketball court. Walk more than two steps with the ball in your hands and you would be called. "Traveling," the ref shouted, sin enough to send the ball to the other team.

A few years later, "trips" would be the sin of choice for many of our generation, trips induced by LSD and other drugs. Sin and travel mixing again, oddly, for they do not usually equate.

Three nights before I began this essay, my wife and I, both in our early 70s, dined at an Indian restaurant. At an adjoining table, a pregnant woman of 20-plus sat with an older couple, maybe her parents, possibly an aunt and uncle. The expectant one was caught up in her condition. "My doctor said I have the most perfect uterus and fallopian tubes he has ever seen," she announced. She spoke proudly of protecting her fetus by using a face mask and gloves when cleaning her cat's litter box. Then she imitated the sounds of her baby's beating heart. "What a trip," she said.

This business of tripping by sin and pregnancy needs

some sorting out, and maybe it takes the wisdom of age to do it. Clearly, some journeys are no longer possible or attractive in later life. The lure of much sin and all pregnancy has passed for many at 65. Maybe that's why the percentage of gray- and white-haired passengers is so high on most ocean cruises. Physical journeys are the best choice left. Go somewhere exotic — that might prove useful practice for the ultimate trip to the great beyond.

But not all of us care to embark by sea. Some of us wish to avoid bobbing about in a metal container packed with several thousand passengers. Others cannot afford the passage. No matter. Travel is a state of mind rather than physical movement.

It's not how far you can get that counts. It's the state of change, the stimulus of the new. Visits to unfamiliar spots in our community or state — or even down the street on foot — may give us fresh perspective. We can be transported by books and music, films and museums, by all the arts. Moving us is what the arts are for. We can be carried away by fresh love, too, and by religion and spirit.

Intentional reach to another person and place, to

unexpected thought and view, to new ideas, to life's deepest mysteries, is the challenge. Connection is the goal.

Travel after 65? Yes. Travel at every age is essential. In fact, that's what life is — a journey through time. The danger is staying still, stultifying, sinning by stasis, and inviting death before it is due. Thousands of travelers go by ticket and passport in their later decades. They have earned both money and leisure, so off they go, across the seas to try out different languages in foreign lands. But exploration is not theirs alone.

I, for my part, travel more widely in spirit than in planes. I attempt to connect with the unknown of others through a camera lens, the unknown of self through writing, the unknown of all through the creative act — a visit with unfolding mystery. I attempt, and sometimes I dare think I succeed.

One of my favorite places for travel is my Unitarian Universalist church, a building and grounds I often visit with camera and pen in hand, a place where I help make music and speak words that at their strongest send others to different places, a spiritual community where I can experience change — a word that for me defines the nature of worship and the nature of travel, too. At church I am moved to the new as I sit in my chair, just as I am moved at home by a book in my lap.

In both these spots I encounter the unexpected — at church, the revealing ideas of a community joined in search of fresh insights and solutions; at home, the engaging stimulus of print or music, of a visiting grandchild, of long and still-evolving love and marriage.

I travel in a theater, too, a high-school theater where I have been privileged for 20-plus years to visit and photograph magical lands made by young casts and crews producing their own new versions of *Godspell*, *The Mikado*, and *Beauty and the Beast*. "Tired and trite," the cynic might say. Oh, no. Look at the spark in the kids' eyes, as dazzling and bright as a nova. I have photographed that spark a thousand times.

There is no one approach for travel that's right for all. What's best for you is whatever floats your boat and carries it wherever you want to go.

The single rule of senior travel is the same as the rule of teen travel — avoid the sin. Or at least avoid repeating the sin. We cannot know the nature of sin without trying it out; we cannot appreciate its price without working up a few bills. That's how we each must discover that senior sin lurks not in going as far as we can get, not in tripping out, but in closing down, achieving inertia on the road by eating at the McDonald's of Hong Kong, or at home by drifting through the televised night. There lies sin, the cardinal sin of snuffing the flame that lights our own life.

Life is like basketball. You have to keep the ball moving — or you'll be called for the wrong kind of travel. The ball will be dead. And so, in spirit, will you.

12

Getting the Most from a Private Tour Guide

by Stephen Wheeler

Stephen Wheeler is a tour organizer and tourism interpreter who lives and works in England, Italy, and Russia. His wife, Natalia, also works in tourism, and they have one child, Leonardo Alexander. Wheeler started his love affair with Italy in 1994 and has lived in Rome, Umbria, Tuscany, and Sardinia. In addition to organizing private tours of central Italy, he writes about visiting Rome on www.ispyrome.com and translates administrative, legal, and cultural documents for private and corporate clients.

Traveling to a different continent is a big deal for anyone, so it's only natural that some feel safer entrusting the booking of flights, hotels, and transfers to a travel agent or cruise line. However, the Internet has unbundled the travel sector, and the young — as well as not-so-young retirees — are now planning their own travels from home. Working with a private guide is one way to reduce the risks involved with do-it-yourself tourism.

As a tour organizer in Rome, I work with many clients who are embarking on Mediterranean cruises. They hire my services because the tours sold by the cruise companies are either for big groups (and are therefore rather impersonal) or are prohibitively expensive. People fly into Rome, see the city, and then take a limo up the coast to meet their cruise ship. The most common mistake guests make is not allowing enough time to see a city that "was not built in a day." Ideally, you need three days to cover the "must see" sights and get over the jet lag. Therefore, my first piece of advice when using a private tour guide is to take it slow; do not take a been-there-seen-it-and-got-the-T-shirt approach.

Private tours by their very definition are customized, and that means the guide and client work together before the tour to build an itinerary that suits your interests and mobility. A good guide will encourage involvement and listen to your needs before you start the tour; if you are not getting this kind of attention, then look elsewhere. When visiting Rome, you don't need a college degree in classics to enjoy hearing about the country's history, architecture, theology, and archaeology, but only a guide brings this all to life. However, if you reach your saturation point, don't be shy about asking your guide to lighten the conversation. A seasoned guide will understand when you need an ice cream, a coffee, or some gift shopping.

Should you be brave enough to organize your whole holiday abroad yourself, then working with a private guide can really be beneficial. Guides know the travel business in their city or region far better than travel agents. Still, do not expect a free lunch — if your guide creates a personalized travel itinerary, especially when there are several cities involved, expect to be asked for a financial commitment in advance of your visit. A recommendation from a guide on a restaurant, hotel, or means of transport can usually be trusted as genuine, as the guide is typically working on a goodwill basis for such referrals. For example, at Enoteca Corsi in Via del Gesù, Rome, my regular lunchtime spot, I don't pay when I take my family there.

A final piece of advice on private tour guides is to try to book them during the midseason — these are the months on either side of the high season (March,

April, October, and November in Rome) — as you will get better terms. For those of you planning to go to central Italy, I've included a courtesy do-it-yourself travel itinerary below.

A week or two in central Italy

3 nights in Rome

Choose a centrally located hotel, bed-and-breakfast, or house rental. Go for authentic locations over watering holes where movie stars may be hanging out, and consider Piazza Navona as the center of the city.

Day 1 — Arrival and orientation in Rome

Most intercontinental flights will get in between 8:00 and 10:00 a.m., but access to your room will usually not be available until 1:00 p.m., so arrange a car transfer, drop your bags at your hotel, and spend the next three to four hours with a guide, seeing the main piazzas and getting orientated. A less expensive option is to go on a hop-on, hop-off bus tour. You need to stay awake until 7:00 or 8:00 p.m. to reduce the effects of jet lag.

Day 2 — Ancient Rome day

An early start is best. You definitely need a guide for this part of your tour to organize advance tickets and illuminate what was once the center of the world's first superpower. Keep the afternoon free for shopping or people watching. Later on, have a night out in the charming Trastevere district.

Day 3 — Vatican day

Get up late, and wander around, revisiting some of the piazzas and fountains. In the afternoon, when it is less busy, go to the Vatican. Now, the line at the Vatican is almost as famous as a certain ceiling painted by Michelangelo. However, the line is only the tip of the iceberg. Meaning, once you get through the line, you still have to face packed galleries. I recommend a 3:00 p.m. entrance time. If you are going on Wednesdays, Fridays, or Saturdays, be sure to buy "skip the queue" tickets by prepurchasing them online from the Vatican Museum's Web site.

Day 4 — Real Italy day

Take a cab to Termini train station and catch a mid-morning local train to Orvieto, which is in Umbria and halfway between Rome and Florence. This historic and picturesque town hits all the expectations of what "real" Italy looks like. The city sits on a cake of rock, and the way up is by cable car. Spend your day doing wine, cheese, and olive-oil tastings, in addition to seeing

Orvieto's world-famous Duomo. Choose a centrally located hotel like Palazzo Piccolomini. The hotel was once a papal palace, and you will find it tough to get a better deal to stay in such a noble facility.

3 nights in Florence
The closer your hotel is to Florence's Duomo, the better it is for you, even though it's easy to get around in this midsize city.

Day 5 — Arrival and orientation in Florence
Catch a morning train for Florence, and on arriving at Firenze S. Maria Novella Station, take a cab to your hotel or just walk it. After getting settled, be sure to go on a guided tour of the city's piazzas in the afternoon.

Day 6 — Art day
Take a guided tour of the Uffizi Gallery and the Accademia, where the *David* is housed. If this is too much art, then just do the Accademia. Florence is the city par excellence for leather shopping — bags, shoes, and gloves. You can always plant the nonshoppers in your group at a café with a bottle of Chianti.

Day 7 — Tuscany activity day
Book a day trip to Tuscany to have a thermal bath at

Montecatini, taste wine in Chianti, do a cooking class, or visit Siena. Even in a bigger group, these tours work well, since once you're on-site you can always peel off and do your own thing.

Day 8 — Head home, or spend another week in Central Italy

Head back to Rome on a high-speed Frecciarossa train. It takes 75 minutes, and you can easily have breakfast at the hotel and still make a 3:00 p.m. flight out of Rome Fiumicino.

If you have another week to stay on vacation, spend seven nights in Tuscany, Umbria, or Northern Lazio (Tuscia) in an *agriturismo* (farmhouse hotel) or a rented villa. Consider doing an activity-based stay, like an Italian-language course or cooking classes. The advantage of a course is that you have a local looking after you, and very often there'll be an organized program of visits to places like Assisi, Greve in Chianti, Gubbio, Lucca, Montcatini, Montalcino, Perugia, Pisa, Siena, Tarquinia, Tuscania, Todi, or Viterbo. If you go it alone, you will need to hire a car or a guide with a car, in order to reach most of these places. My own little corner of Italian *paradiso* is the Island of Giglio off the Tuscan coast — one day I will retire there.

Section

THERE'S SUCH A LOT
OF WORLD TO SEE

13

The Let's-Sell-Our-House-and-See-the-World Retirement Plan

by Lynne Martin

In 2010, Lynne Martin and her husband, Tim, a novelist, sold their house, ditched most of their belongings, packed their suitcases, and became international nomads. Martin's blog, homefreeadventures.com, which chronicles their nomadic life, has over 2,000 followers, and her article in *The Wall Street Journal*, on the cover of the "Next" section, was one of the most popular of all time. People like their idea.

Born in Texas and reared in Chicago, Martin studied journalism, and after working in radio and television, she founded Maynor and Associates, a public relations firm in Hollywood. She wrote a book about her life as a senior gypsy called *Home Sweet Home Anywhere: How We Sold Our House, Created a New Life, and Saw the World*.

The Martins have four daughters and seven grandchildren.

"If you're going to live with a woman in a 500- square-foot apartment for two months surrounded by hostile natives, you'd better really *like* her," my husband, Tim, said in response to a question about what we've learned since embarking on our home-free lifestyle.

Our home is wherever we and our 30-inch suitcases are. In short, we're senior gypsies, and we've learned a lot about life and each other on the road. In early 2011, we sold our house in California and moved the objects we treasured into a 10-by-15-foot storage unit. Since then, we have lived in furnished apartments and houses in Mexico, Argentina, Florida, Turkey, France, Italy, Ireland, and Morocco. Plans for Portugal, Germany, South America, Asia, Australia, and New Zealand are in the works, and we intend to keep traveling until the wheels fall off.

When we retired, we bought a home near our children and planned to live a predictable life, with Tim writing novels and both of us enjoying the garden, our grandchildren, and community involvement. After three years of that idyllic existence, we knew it just wasn't enough for us. We had to find a way to experience the world in more than three-week vacation bites, to live like locals for at least a month at a time in places that intrigued us. Tim and I knew, at 65 and 70 years old respectively, that we couldn't delay. Our health was excellent and our energy levels high, so we had to implement the plan right away. In order to afford putting down new roots one country at a time, we would have to sell our house and let the capital help finance our wanderlust. Things worked out quickly. Within four months, we kissed our children and friends good-bye and set off for Mexico and Argentina on the first leg of our new life.

As I write this we are living in an Irish apartment, which is a small part of an elegant Georgian mansion, built circa 1712. We look out our tall windows across lovely old trees dressed for autumn, with the wild Irish Sea dancing in the distance. Arriving in Dublin presented us with challenges we have come to expect: *Where is the closest grocery market? How does the washing machine work? Is there good parking at the railway station? What was that Wi-Fi password again?* We are convinced that solving those and a thousand other puzzles keeps us resilient and sharper than we ever were at home. Sometimes, our flexible life is exhausting, but it's never dull.

After living in other people's spaces without a home base for some time, we've had the chance to take stock and to learn things about each other — and ourselves

— that surprised us. I'd like to share four of these discoveries with you:

It's Not About Money

Seeing flocks of seagulls form a living wreath around the Blue Mosque is our fondest memory of Istanbul. When Paris comes to mind, I think of walking along the Seine, gaping at those glorious golden sculptures on the bridge. Dodging puddles and laughing with robed shopkeepers during a surprise deluge in Marrakech will always be my favorite impression of that fantastic city. Here's the thing: all of those experiences are free to every visitor, no matter what their budget. They are the thrilling moments that make Tim and me want to keep on traveling!

Time Is the Greatest Luxury

We did not expect that our lifestyle would give us permission to fritter away time. Now, that's not quite as shallow as it sounds. Since we spend a month or two in each location, we can see the sights at a leisurely pace; in fact, we savor the trips to and from a museum or monument almost as much as the visits themselves. But there are some days when we simply stay at home in our jammies, do a little laundry, and read or watch

TV, just as we would at home. We need downtime. Going to the movies in the afternoon and just plain goofing around for a day are things we do whether we're in London, San Miguel de Allende, Mexico, or Paso Robles, California, and we have enough time in each place to relax and enjoy without tourist guilt! It's been quite a revelation.

Be Prepared to Make Mistakes

Do not think for a moment that every day is perfect. We meet with all kinds of adversity — lousy weather, bad travel days, spotty Internet connections, unpleasant people, colds, scary drivers, dirty apartments, mean tourists, and our own bad moods. We have our "moments" when we snip and snarl at each other, and we certainly do not agree about everything. But being home-free has taught us to forgive quickly and move on down the road together.

We've made notable mistakes, and we've corrected them because we think life is too short to be unhappy. We left our Buenos Aires apartment two weeks early, taking a hit on the rent, because the city had simply worn us out; we fled Florence because six weeks of soaring temperatures made us miserable; we've skipped prepaid performances because we were too tired to go; and we've canceled some flights even though they cost us money. We've learned that our health and sanity are more important than the budget. We can recover money, but not time.

We Like Each Other!

Our unique retirement plan works for one simple reason: we really *like* each other. Of course, we *love* each other deeply and always have. The surprise is that even with the challenges of our nomadic existence, living in some very tight places, and sometimes having no one else around for days at a time who speaks our language, we still prefer each other's company above anyone else's. Our conversations remain lively and challenging, and even after all these years we can make each other burst out laughing with delight and surprise. Our children sometimes accuse us of being a cult with only two members. They are close to the truth, and the cult's password is love!

14

What Retirees Can Learn from Career Breakers

by Jeff Jung

Known as "The Career Break Travel Guy," Jeff Jung is the author of *The Career Break Traveler's Handbook*, hosts the global TV show, *The Career Break Travel Show*, and blogs at http://CareerBreakSecrets.com. An international traveler since his first trip to Australia at the age of 16, his career break made him a true citizen of the world. He left a consulting-turned-corporate-marketing career to learn Spanish fluently in South America, to see magnificent sunsets and sunrises in far-flung places like the Galapagos, Easter Island, Cappadocia, and the Nile River, and to learn to ski (at the age of 36!).

As people's relationship towards their work has changed, a new phenomenon in the battle for work-life balance has emerged: the "career break." For many, this means taking time in life to focus their passion and energy on themselves, rather than on their career. While some consider it a mini retirement, I don't. Career breakers just want a break — 70 percent of them go back to the career they had before.

Because taking a break requires planning, preparation, and fortitude, career breakers want to make their time count. They don't want their time to be wasted lying around. They usually have one major goal they want to accomplish, along with a list of secondary and tertiary goals. As a result, they are active travelers seeking "real" experiences and connections. While the definition of "real" is subjective, they travel differently than they ever have before: independently, intently, and with great curiosity.

When I look at the current generation of retirees and those about to retire (mostly people in my inner circle of friends and family), I see those same qualities shine. Not all want to travel the world, but they are hardly homebodies. While they are always happy to spend time with their grandchildren, they aren't sitting around waiting for the next call from their kids asking for babysitting services.

As you consider how you will spend your time during your retirement, here are three useful ideas from the career-break travel world. While career breakers play tourist as they explore different cities, these activities are what help give meaning to their journey. Through them, they discover the world and learn a little bit more about themselves.

Volunteer and Give Back

While filming in South Africa, I met Peter, a 53-year-old pharmaceutical sales executive. He and his wife were volunteering at Cotlands, an HIV/AIDS orphanage and community development center in Johannesburg, South Africa, as part of their career break.

"Why did you decide to take a break at this point of your career?" I asked. "I mean, aren't you concerned about getting a job when you go back?"

Peter looked up at me and smiled. "Well, last year, after I turned 52, I had a heart attack. I always wanted to take a sabbatical to see the world. But, I always put it off. 'Tomorrow's another day, and I can think about it then,' I told myself. After my heart attack, I realized that tomorrow is not guaranteed."

Peter and his wife spent six months volunteering at Cotlands and an additional six months driving from South Africa up eastern Africa to Uganda and back. At

Cotlands, Peter and his wife applied their professional skills to develop business plans and identify new products to sell to help the organization generate additional revenue streams, so that it could be less reliant on donations.

Lesson learned: Just like Peter and his wife, you have skills that organizations can use. The best experiences occur when there's a match between what the organization needs and the skills you have a passion to share.

Learn Something New

Career breaks are the perfect time for people to pursue a hobby that has been neglected or to pick up a new skill like photography, cooking, writing, or learning a foreign language.

"Okay, Jeff," said my ski instructor, *"voy a quitar los bastones* (I'm going to take away your ski poles)."

Gulp.

One of my goals on my career break was to learn to ski. I didn't grow up skiing, and at 36, I wasn't so sure I could learn. As I was already in Argentina studying Spanish, I made my way to Bariloche, a picturesque ski town in the Andes at the northern tip of the Patagonia region. Watching the five-year-olds go down the slopes fearlessly while I battled in a herky-jerky fashion to keep from falling was a humbling experience. Recognizing my overreliance on my ski poles and underreliance on the movement of my hips, my ski instructor took my poles. Then, with his back to the bottom of the mountain, he faced me and folded his arms. Holding onto him, we skied down the mountain together. At some point along the way, I learned to rely on my hips to control my movements — and to relax as I went downhill. I may never ski the expert black-diamond runs, but at least I know how to get off the gondola without falling and to make my way down the slope . . . and enjoy it.

Lesson learned: We are never too old to pursue our dreams or learn something new. If you have the drive and a willing attitude, now is a great time to be a student again.

See the World in Cool Ways

There are so many ways to see and experience the world — whether by hiking, biking, or taking a ferry. It doesn't have to be by plane or by shuttle bus. On a career break, as in retirement, you have more time to explore the options available. Instead of flying around Europe, why not take the train? While in Patagonia, why not take a four-day ferry ride through the protected fjords of the southern Chilean coast to see a part of the world few do? While in Spain, why not make the pilgrimage walking all or part of the Way of St. James known as the Camino de Santiago?

The travel possibilities vary. I once met a career breaker who was visiting the top paragliding places around the world. Another time, I encountered a couple of best friends who decided that they wanted to "chase summer" by scuba diving around the world.

Lesson learned: Packaged tours have their value and place. But there are so many other options for all budgets that will allow you to create your own path, your own itinerary. Whether you have always been an independent soul or not, with just a little research you can discover strategies to explore destinations in an unusual way.

15

Gap Years Are Wasted on the Young

by Jo Carroll

Jo Carroll decided that 30 years working in Child Protective Services was long enough. She had earned her gap year. She set off with little more than curiosity and an armful of notebooks, and returned with more stories than could be told in a month. She wrote about her adventures in her book *Over the Hill and Far Away*, which has been successful on both sides of the Atlantic. An e-book is available about her subsequent trip to Nepal. She welcomes visits to her Web site (www.jocarroll.co.uk), where you can find more of her writing, photos from her trips, and links to her books.

One New Year's Eve, six years ago, I was staying in a national park in a southern corner of Nepal. There was an Indian family in the neighboring hut, and we were sitting together round a huge bonfire trying to keep warm. Elephants, who had carried us into the jungle earlier that day, shuffled in their enclosure nearby. Somewhere, a leopard roared.

Then the music started, pipes and drums and Eastern rhythms that echoed in the cold night air. An older woman in a blue sari, orange cardigan, and pink gloves pulled me to my feet, and we began to dance. I had no idea what to do, but — with women on each side of me — I managed to sway round and round the fire with them until we were all happily panting, clutching our stomachs to catch a breath.

Then a man turned to me and asked, "Why are you traveling?"

"For nights like this," I told him.

I'd wanted to travel since my teens. But life — in the form of education, and work, and family — got in the way. A headline in the newspaper startled me out of the rhythm of days that had grown comfortable: "Gap Years Are Wasted on the Young." I nodded, in a wise way (as we do when we are older and know better); the benefits of travel need maturity if they are to be enjoyed to the fullest.

I'm not sure my daughters were convinced that packing a rucksack in my late 50s was evidence of maturity. I gave up my job, sold my car, found a tenant for my house, and took off for a year — on my own, landing first in Australia and New Zealand, where at least everyone spoke the same language, before launching into the Indian subcontinent and then to the delights of the Far East. My grown-up gap year. A glorious interruption in life's predictabilities.

There was planning — of sorts. I spent hours poring over guidebooks, working out where to go next, where to stay, where to eat. I always knew where I was going to sleep for the next few days. I stayed in hostels to begin with: they are great places for meeting people, and indulging in the 'where are you from' conversations that are the lifeblood of traveling (and I met some fascinating people). In more unruly places, I found hotels: it was easier to keep clean in them, but they lacked the camaraderie of hostels.

I hadn't realized that this was something older women rarely do on their own. I met older couples. Spending the kids' inheritance, they told me. Many stayed in luxury resorts, dipping their toes into the local culture, and retreating for spa treatments and five-star meals, lucky people. Some of the older men were sorry souls, searching for company only among the young and beautiful. But many shared my unquenchable curiosity about the wonderful world around us. Where were the single women? I met women working with charities, doing great work to make life better for the disabled and disadvantaged. I didn't meet any "going walkabout" as I was.

Yet, gap-year traveling for grown-ups is such fun! Just because we have a few gray hairs and our bodies are prone to wobbling doesn't mean we have lost our enthusiasm. We might not have the energy we had once; we don't need it. While the young race between bungee jumping and white-water rafting, we sip ginger tea and chat with the waiters — often students longing to practice their English. We understand that the world can be a dangerous place, but that makes it easier to keep ourselves safe. Do we take a shortcut down a narrow passageway to reach a nightclub? Of course not; we'd rather sit somewhere, busy with a beer, and watch the world go by.

Tempted to try it yourself? Of course you are. So, where do you begin?

You need to attend to practicalities; they are boring but can make or break a trip. You'll want to be sure you have locking luggage that isn't too heavy. That your travel insurance covers everything you need it to cover. That you have all possible inoculations. That someone will look after (or live in) your house. That you have the technology you need to keep in touch with those you love — a mobile phone that works all over the world, and e-mail addresses. You need to think about money. There are ATMs in almost all big cities now. But it's worth having dollars with you if you plan to go off the beaten track, plus make sure to have some way of getting hold of money in a hurry should you need it.

When should you go? There is no right answer. For many, a "golden gap year" is a bridge between the rigors of work and the realities of retirement. You might decide to buy flight tickets before your retirement savings plan kicks in. Or you may need a year or so to clear your head of work before setting off. Your gap year can be whatever you need it to be — and whenever you need to do it.

What you don't need is permission from your family and friends. This is your grown-up decision, and you can make it for yourself. I was fortunate. My daughters have cheered me wherever I've been — although there were many escapades I didn't tell them about until I got home. But there were others who muttered: *Wasn't I a bit old for this? Shouldn't I have grown up by now? What if I was mugged, or caught a terrible disease, or was incurably lonely?* I shrugged it all off. Had I listened to all the contrary advice I've been given, I'd never have left my front door.

Of course, it was life changing. I have walked in streets most people only see on television. I know what the temples in India smell like. I recognize the roar of a leopard. I have friends on five continents.

It's within your reach, too. The hard part is making the decision to go: then let the excitement begin.

And no, I haven't stopped. Why spend the winter in the cold and wet, when I can catch a plane to Bangkok?

16

Start with Your "A" List

by Michael Jeans

Michael D. Jeans is president of New Directions, Inc., a nationally recognized career-management firm in Boston that helps senior executives and professionals develop new jobs, start new ventures, and find alternatives to full-time employment (or full-time retirement). Previously, Jeans was president and CEO of Roxy.com, Inc., an online retailer of consumer electronics. Earlier, he was CEO of Nashua Photo, Inc., and president of Wesson/Peter Pan Foods (a division of ConAgra). He has a B.A. from the College of the Holy Cross, graduating *magna cum laude*, and an M.B.A. from the Tuck School of Business at Dartmouth College. Jeans is a director of AMICA Mutual Insurance Company. He also serves on the Board of Directors of the Boys & Girls Club of Greater Nashua (New Hampshire) and the Boston Minuteman Council of the Boy Scouts of America.

I believe that travel in retirement is a terrific way to attack your bucket list. But before I go any further, I want to delete three words from the prior sentence: *retirement* and *bucket list*. "Retirement" because it conjures up all the wrong meanings for today's active and engaged people when they reach

65. The word means "to retreat" or "to go to bed." A recent study showed that retired people watch an average of 47 hours of TV a week. Boring! Get rid of the word. "Bucket list" because it sounds so . . . terminal. I suggest we substitute "curious list" instead. I believe that we should put travel destinations on our "curious lists" because travel can lead to discovering new interests, cultivating a hobby, learning, planning subsequent trips, and just making us more interesting as people! Incorporate travel into what you do in your 60s, 70s, and 80s. Mix it up with adventure travel (while you're physically able), family trips, and going to places where you can just relax.

My wife just retired from her job two years ago. I'm still working, but we have decided to step up our travel. In the last two years, we have gone to Aruba, the Arctic, Africa, and Austria. An unintentional alliterative coincidence led us to call this our "A" list. (It has also caused us to wonder whether we'll ever plan a trip to Abilene or Amesbury!)

A quick look at these destinations can highlight some of the great things that we have learned about travel.

Aruba. In Aruba, we own a timeshare. We go there

every February. We read books on the beach, watch the sun set, and frequent several restaurants we like a lot. It's comfortable. We know what to expect. It's part of our travel rhythm that we look forward to. We come back recharged and refreshed. It has a definite place in our annual travel plans.

Arctic Circle. Have you traveled into the Arctic Circle (not Antarctica at the South Pole, but the Arctic up near the North Pole)? We never knew anyone who had ever made such a trip. That was part of the attraction for us. It was an adventure . . . with reputed spectacular scenery and a fascinating history and story to tell. We planned this vacation because we happened to get a flyer in the mail from a summer environmental camp that our kids had attended years ago. The camp was putting together this exploratory trip to the Arctic and was offering it to the parents of the campers. It was in September. My wife had just retired from her career as a school teacher. If she wasn't going to the classroom in September, where would she go? She convinced me to try the Arctic. It was NEVER on any bucket list of ours, but we were mildly curious. We had a connection to the camp. We decided to have an adventure. What a good decision! We traveled aboard a Russian expedition ship (never to be confused with a luxury liner) and debarked daily on Zodiac® rafts to hike and explore terrain and Inuit villages. We gained a unique understanding about a spectacularly beautiful part of our earth (including polar bears), saw firsthand the reality of global warming around the polar ice caps, and learned the fascinating geopolitical history of how countries have established settlements in the northland.

Africa. I bet that you've known a lot of people who have safaried in Africa. You may have done this yourself (or have it on your "curious list"). We enjoyed a terrific safari in Tanzania with another couple who are close friends. But the driving force was not the safari (great as it was). Our friends are deeply involved with Save the Children, the international organization that does such great work in the developing world to improve the lot of children and families in need. Before our safari, we spent a week in the far backcountry of Mozambique visiting Save the Children projects and trying to lend a hand. The shocking poverty and miserable health and educational situation gave us a vividly personal grasp of the enormity of the "African problem." It stands in stark contrast to the touristy beauty of safari life and the astounding close-up views of elephants, monkeys, and lions. It got us thinking about how/when we can return to Africa someday with our kids. It also has made us advocates for the work of Save the Children and curious about how, when I eventually do retire from my current job, we can get more involved.

Austria. I cycle to keep fit. My wife (who keeps fit in other ways) has not been a cyclist. I found a bicycling trip to Austria (and Slovenia and Italy) that some friends of ours raved about. Biking in Europe is a great way to slow down, see the countryside, travel rural back roads, and meet the locals in a way that we never could when traveling on a tour bus. This time, I convinced my wife to go. It was a wonderful adventure. It required some degree of fitness but not a lot. Hey, the average age of the 18 people on our bike-tour group was 64!

Lessons abound from this trip. First, we were open to looking into this type of trip when our friends said, "You gotta do this!" Second, my wife and I needed to both agree and be flexible and sensitive to what the other wanted to do. My wife (who is a real trouper) told me she'd try a biking vacation if I really wanted to do it. Three days into the trip, she turned to me and said,

"I'm glad we did this." (Note: We just booked another biking trip to France next fall!) I am sure that she will be proposing to me shortly that we go on a garden tour or museum tour. I promise I'll be flexible.

When you retire (there's that word again!), try to add travel into your schedule. View it as relaxation and also as a continuous learning experience that keeps you mentally and physically fit. Make a plan. Be spontaneous. Be flexible. Be curious. Have fun. Meanwhile, we are chipping away at our "A" list. We are planning a trip to Australia next year. We are wondering when we will eventually get to Zanzibar.

17

Unconventional Travelers

by Janet and Ed Howle

Ed and Janet Howle aren't really retired but fit the category by being well over 65. Currently, they consider themselves novelists. Both Ed and Janet have had several other careers, none of which contributed to their decision to write fiction. It has been their life experiences that provide material for their writing. Their debut novel, *The Long Road to Paris*, is based on their around-the-world antique-car rally, travels in Asia, and years of living in Paris. In addition, they are avid ocean sailors. Their novel-in-progress is set on a sailboat in the Bahamas. At this point in their lives, they divide their time between their home in North Carolina, sailing, and international travel.

Jan: We've never been what most people would call conventional travelers. Just this year, as I turned 67 and before Ed turned 78, we sailed our 31-foot sailboat to the Bahamas, drove our 1967 VW Beetle from New York to Alaska in the Trans-American antique-car rally, and rented an apartment in Paris for a month while attending a writer's workshop. If we don't have a reason to travel, we invent one.

Almost as soon as we met, I knew my life would include travel and adventure. Ed is, and always has been, a restless person. Age has not changed that. He's at his best with serendipitous travel, and at his worst when life requires routine. Before we married, Ed had already crossed the Atlantic in a sailboat and was planning to sail around the world with his three children. We spent our honeymoon sailing off the coast of North Carolina, in a storm — not the worst one we would encounter (that one would occur in the Caribbean years later), but bad enough to make me think we might have the shortest marriage on record. Now, 36 years and three sailboats later, both the sailing and the marriage have stood the test of time.

Travel for us had to include children if we were going to travel before retirement. We were not young parents when we adopted a family of three more children. We (make that Ed) decided it was time to buy a larger sailboat, homeschool the youngest two boys, and sail the Bahamas. Life on a sailboat requires everyone to focus on the moment. Play, learning, and work merged into one and bonded our family. This worked well for three consecutive winters; then the day came when the boys put friends and sports ahead of parents.

Back home, Ed could not return to a nine-to-five schedule. Fortunately, by this time our jobs were portable, so when he woke up at night, as he is prone to do, and suggested we move to Paris with the boys, I could at least ponder it. Now understand, we spoke no French and had never lived or raised children in a large city. Details should never stop a good idea, so we moved, planning to stay a year. After *five* years, we finally returned to the United States.

If I were inclined to give advice (which generally I'm not, although our kids may tell you otherwise), I would recommend living abroad. There are many ways to do this. Recently, I met a couple who will retire next year, and their plan is to live in a different country one month of each year that follows. It takes an open mind to live in another county, but anyone who takes on this challenge will accumulate never-ending adventures and lifelong memories. It broadens your perspective and understanding of other people, and most important. you'll learn about yourself. Life will be different — not better, not worse, just different. The adventure of living in Paris not only included the city itself, but put us in the proximity of other fabulous places. Traveling by car and train, we visited Barcelona, Rome, Brussels, London, and Munich, just to name a few.

Ed: Jan would have you believe that I am the one who has instigated all our travel adventures. That's not entirely true. Antique-car rallying is another travel mode we enjoy, and Jan was the one who discovered an around-the-world antique-car rally from New York to Paris scheduled for 2008. We made it fit into our life plan. Unfortunately, that rally was canceled when China withdrew our travel permits. However, this led us to still another adventure and more travel while we waited for that rally to be reorganized.

We had planned to write a travel memoir of this unique experience, but we ultimately put that book on hold. Preferring not to be constrained by telling only the facts of our personal story, we fictionalized the world rally in our first novel, *The Long Road to Paris*. We had never written fiction, and while the story is equal parts love and suspense, the setting is based on our own travel adventures. One thing was missing: part of the novel includes scenes of traveling across

Siberia and Russia, and Jan felt we could not write an authentic description of this without experiencing it ourselves. She jumped on the Internet and soon we were onboard the Golden Eagle Trans-Siberian Express, a 15-day train trip along the Trans-Siberian Railway from Vladivostok to Moscow.

This was perhaps closer to a cruise ship or bus tour than we had ever done; we had our own cabin and a Russian-speaking guide. But we had a specific goal for our trip: to add an accurate depiction of life in Siberia to our novel. We could not have seen as much of this vast country more quickly than by train. We have ridden trains throughout Europe, but Jan wasn't particularly enthusiastic about taking a Russian train; everything we read had made it sound anything but charming. But our purpose was research, and so we persevered. Our train dipped into Mongolia, around the shores of Lake Baikal, to Novosibirsk, and to Ekaterinburg, where Czar Nicholas II and his family were executed. We saw historic sights firsthand but, most important, we experienced daily life in Siberia.

The around-the-world rally was finally rescheduled in 2011, and we drove our 1967 VW Beetle from New

York City west to Paris, crossing three continents and covering 14,000 miles. We discovered that China has both the worst and best roads in the world, and that we can't read road signs with Chinese characters or Cyrillic letters. By this time, Jan was blogging daily, and that travel adventure, along with others since then, is described on our blog, www.thelongroadtoparis. wordpress.com. Now we are planning our next travel adventure on our new, larger sailboat, *Sable*. We leave for the Bahamas as soon as hurricane season is over, and we will spend two months or more island-hopping.

Ed and Jan: Perhaps our way of travel will not appeal to you, but there is one aspect of planning and traveling that should interest anyone at any age. You will learn about yourself. Travel will stretch your comfort zone and provide constant mental challenges. You find you must be flexible, curious, tolerant, accepting of whatever the day brings, and willing to test your problem-solving abilities and patience. It keeps you young so that you can live until you die. We hope to meet you on the road, somewhere, sometime.

18

Change Through Travel — It's Easier Than You Think

by Christine T. Mackay

Christine T. Mackay, cofounder and executive director of Crooked Trails, a nonprofit community-based travel organization, has dedicated her life to working and volunteering in environmental education, outdoor recreation, community development, and ecotourism. She cofounded and directed Bearfoot Backpacker, offering outdoor educational excursions around Washington State. But her love of international travel, and her concern about the negative effects of tourism on culture and environment, led her to cofound Crooked Trails in 1998.

Mackay's ability to engage and impassion audiences about the environment and tourism has led to speaking engagements at clubs, international conferences, bookstores, universities and schools.

Whatʼs it like to travel with a purpose?

In reality, everyone does this, whether they are relaxing on the beaches of Hawaii, going on safari in South Africa, seeing the Eiffel Tower, or spending time with friends. Often, however, to "travel with a purpose" conjures up thoughts of deeper, more meaningful experiences. In other words, rather than getting away from it all, the traveler chooses to *engage* with it all. How many of us have headed to some tropical paradise to lounge on the beach, drink a fruity cocktail, and see a few sights, but returned home utterly the same person as before — albeit with a tan? Traveling with a purpose means traveling *with the intent to be changed.*

I recently offered a lecture and slide show on volunteer tourism, where every person in the audience was at least 60 years old. People did not come for a respite from the rain, or the free coffee and cookies; they were all seriously engaged in researching what meaningful travel was all about. Most assumed that it would involve a certain amount of service. There is no question that traveling abroad to offer your services to those in need is indeed meaningful. However, there are other ways to have a transformative experience beyond digging holes or building the walls of a school.

Over the past decade, I have taken travelers to a wide range of destinations on trips they said changed their lives. What happened that made them feel so different? Often the travel programs involved service projects, such as building a school in Nepal or smokeless ovens in Peru, and the meaning in that is clear. But many times, the focus of the trip was simply to meet and understand the local people while traveling in a responsible and sustainable manner (making sure the tourist dollars stay in the communities where they are spent, and that respect for cultural ways is practiced). By and large, the most fulfilling moments in our travels occur when we engage with the locals. This doesn't mean to see and photograph them, but to actually *meet* them.

Last year on a trip to Nepal, I remember one man telling me — after having just spent the previous year going around the world — that in all his travels he had never been in a village where he actually met the people living there. He had gone on dozens of tours in cities, seeing one amazing sight after another, but in all that time, he never interacted with a local person. Yet, in one special week in the village of Chandeni in Nepal, he had talked with — and shared food with — at least a hundred of the villagers. He worked next to them during the day to build a school for the village.

During breaks, he had kids clamoring to sit on his lap, which brought tears to his eyes since he knew that in a few short months he would be a father for the first time. Every morning, he would sit at the small hearth watching his housemother cook the morning meal of sweetened, spiced milk tea and lentils and rice. He danced and laughed with villagers who had come to "meet the American" and thank him. At the end of six days he had changed. Why? Because it's relationships that change us, not places.

We may be moved by a place, but sharing stories and experiences with others helps us to see the world from their point of view, thus altering the way we see ourselves and our place in the world. In fact, it changes how we see and experience the world itself. Yet, we often shy away from this when we travel, engaging only with those who are in our own group. We all need to find a way to reach out beyond ourselves, overcoming our shyness or our fear of those who are different. It's important that we not only appreciate others, but learn to *share* ourselves with them.

How do you do this? First, choose a place that calls to you; perhaps it's going on safari in Kenya. Then, take some time to research the people and issues. Perhaps you are interested in the problem facing many Kenyan children: lack of education. Look into NGOs (non-governmental organizations) that work in that location on that issue. Contact them about the possibility of your volunteering or donating to their cause.

If working with an NGO is out of your realm, then simply open up to those assisting you in your tour: the taxi driver, the person at the front desk of the hotel, the guide, etc. I remember talking all the time with my Zulu safari guide in South Africa, and it led to my entire group being invited to his village, where we met many members of his family. Eventually, we all committed to building them a house. I remember how moved I was when three months later I received the photos of the grateful family in the house. This is traveling with a purpose. The purpose is to engage with those we meet and to be changed forever because of it. It's a two-way street, and the give and take of travel is what makes it so worthwhile.

19

We Traveled the World for Two Years, Enhancing Our Lives with More Adventure and Romance

by Wayne and Pat Dunlap

Wayne and Pat Dunlap are travel TV hosts of *Plan Your Escape*™ and travel columnists for the Huffington Post. Hostelbookers. com selected them as among "The Best Baby Boomer Travel Bloggers to Follow." They are members of the exclusive Travelers' Century Club, and have visited 100 countries, taking planes, cars, trains, buses, and organized tours. Stories about their adventures have appeared in *The Christian Science Monitor*, *Entrepreneur Magazine*, and SecondAct. Their popular Web site is http://UnhookNow.blogspot.com.

Travel tops the dream list for boomers in a recent AARP national survey. Almost all of us have a bucket list of travel dreams.

My wife, Pat, and I, both now 62 years old, have been

fortunate to share a life-changing adventure together. Recently, we rented out our home in San Diego, California, and traveled the world for two years. In that time, we ventured to 51 countries, making a grand total of 100 countries on six continents and 44 U.S. states that we've visited in our lifetime.

Years ago, we gave up careers in the high-tech industry to start our own business so we could devote more time to our son and doing some traveling. With the normal joys and obligations of our business, raising a family, and volunteer work, our vacations were limited to two to three weeks and were finished way too soon.

We had worked continuously since graduating from college. When we sold our business and became empty nesters in 2009, we both had other new business ideas. I suggested to Pat that we take a few months off to travel before we launched into something new. We had always dreamed about exploring some of our dream destinations, such as the Greek Isles, Italy's beautiful Lake District, Croatia's Dalmatian coastline, New Zealand, the Panama Canal, and other places.

After considering my suggestion, Pat came back a few days later with a bolder plan and suggested that we take a whole year off. My first thought was, "Americans can't take a year off!" But being a former economics professor, I did some research and discovered a slightly different way to travel the world for less than the cost of living at home. I learned that we could travel for months for the same amount that we normally spent on our vacations — less than $100 per day for both of us combined — just by eliminating expenses. So, off we went on our world adventure.

Travel has permanently improved our lives, giving us a renewed outlook. We learned much more about ourselves and what makes us happy. By taking time away from our routines, we were able to reevaluate what was working for us and what wasn't.

Traveling with only a suitcase has shown us that we need less material things to be happy. We have discovered that it is much more important to slow down and enjoy people, friends, new experiences, adventures, romance, and learning.

Meeting a Canadian couple on a cruise developed into a longstanding relationship (we've stayed with them in Vancouver and joined them on a tour of Egypt, where we all climbed the Great Pyramid).

We are having fun, laughing and waking up excited every day about having the experience we choose. Life without routines is inspiring and renews your playful spirit and love of life. Through our many adventures — which have included riding an elephant in Bali, river rafting in Argentina, climbing the Great Wall of China, sailboating on the Nile River, staying in a Bedouin camp in the Jordanian desert, visiting the hillside tribes in Thailand, scuba diving in the Red Sea, and zip-lining through a Costa Rican rain forest — we learned that there is so much more to life than we ever imagined.

One day in New Zealand, we were in crampons, hiking a massive glacier of blue ice. Another day, we were in swimsuits, savoring wine and cheese in the churning, Jacuzzi-like waters where two rivers converged.

You have a chance to enhance your relationship when traveling. If you want to find the spice of life, make each trip an adventure. You'll have so much to talk about and you'll have such great memories, too. You'll rediscover the things that attracted you to each other in the first place, when you experience new cities and activities as a couple. Traveling the world has brought us closer together.

A cooking lesson in Thailand allowed us to discover a whole new world of flavor that we love today. Eating healthy and taking care of each other is another benefit of rediscovery and partner appreciation.

Now Pat and I have a new "career." We love to inspire others to travel, helping them to safely realize and afford their travel dreams — from weekend getaways to longer vacations. Our mission in life is to help people live their travel dreams without breaking the bank. We look forward to sharing inspiring travel ideas, powerful how-to tips, and unique bargain-finding strategies with you on our Plan Your Escape™ World Travel Adventure blog, UnhookNow.com, and our TV show, *Plan Your Escape,*™ is on the CW Network.

Traveling is easier, safer, and more affordable than you may believe. We encourage everyone to go out and see this great big beautiful world. The experience has greatly enhanced our lives. See you on the road!

20

Never a Still Moment

by Leyla Giray Alyanak

Leyla Giray Alyanak has spent nearly four decades as a journalist and development worker with a passion for travel and improving people's lives in developing countries. On her solo travels, she has found time to get lost in a Mozambican minefield, paddle her way out of a flood in the Philippines, and get stampeded by an elephant cow in Nigeria. Born in Paris and raised around the world, she writes a popular Web site for traveling women (www.women-on-the-road.com) and has published *Women on the Road*, an e-book for baby-boomer women who want to travel independently.

Travel has always been my life, from my first voyage on the Orient-Express at the age of five weeks until today. Solo travel wasn't something I chose. It chose me. At 15, I was living in Spain with my family and decided to discover North Africa — so I just went. My parents were unappreciative of my newfound explorations and brought me home. Having tasted the freedom of owning my own life, I would rarely stay put after that. For fun, study, or my career, I always wanted to be on the move, and so I would be. I even worked in fields guaranteed to keep me traveling: journalism, public relations, and international development for the United Nations.

At the age of 43, I decided none of this was enough. I had few ties — an unpleasant relationship, no children, a family who already lived across the world — so I shed the few that remained. I gave up my job, the car, the apartment, and I set off to Cape Town with a one-way ticket. I planned on traveling around Africa for six months. I was gone for nearly four years.

This was before the Internet and the cell phone. I was able to e-mail by using a bulky modem — it was the mid-90s, after all — but there were few recipients at the other end. A friend back home printed my e-mails and posted them to everyone in my circle. Not too high-tech, but effective. I phoned my family with international calling cards from phone booths, and in some countries, like Burma, I couldn't call at all.

We were still a relatively rare and intrepid breed: we solo women backpackers. We were of all ages and sizes and colors, but we shared a desire — no, a *need* — to discover the world, person by person, village by village. I would run into backpackers who had barely finished school, as well as 80-year-olds who were pushing their way across continents as best they could, sometimes aided by a cane, often at a faster clip than mine, and always fueled by the hunger for discovery. The wonderful travel writer Dervla Murphy even crossed my path.

We all became friends, our common thread being "the road." I remember a few weeks into my Africa trip, I was in the back of a minibus in KwaZulu-Natal. A girl from New Zealand nonchalantly said that she'd been "on the road" for two years. I thought to myself, *How could you travel for that long?* I would soon discover just how easy it is for months to stretch into years.

There were funny moments — an impromptu invitation to a Balinese wedding; floating down a river in Thailand wearing only my sarong, to general hilarity; almost starting a diplomatic incident by refusing a traditional alcoholic drink in Laos; and lying on the floor in a Filipino jeepney and being smuggled into a local wedding (and then being stranded there by a flood, having to pay to chop down a tree, build a canoe, and paddle out with the local priest).

There were also difficult moments, as with everything in life. I sat at a crossroads for two full days with a hurt knee in northern Uganda, waiting for a bus with an empty seat to appear. I was robbed of some money by someone I trusted. In Kenya one night, loneliness just swept over me like a tidal wave, nailing me to my damp bed, which sagged in the equatorial heat. I almost drowned in Zanzibar, having for a moment forgotten I couldn't swim.

Those low points quickly faded from memory as I gathered new experiences and friends: high-school students looking for English-language practice in Sumatra and Turkey. A Zimbabwean football team on Lake Como. Eating flowers surrounded by South African vineyards. Watching the sun set over Venice on my way to a Vivaldi concert. Crossing a patch of the Amazon with indigenous people whose language I couldn't understand. Sneaking into Burma before the doors opened wide.

Every memory remains pristine, some older, some so recent I can still smell and taste them.

An unexpected benefit of solo travel was that I grew increasingly self-sufficient and self-confident, since all problems had to be solved on the spot, whether I spoke the language or not. Solo travel also brought me greater tolerance, especially for the little things like tardiness and inefficiency and lumpy beds. The rest of the world didn't work to my clock, I found out, and no amount of fretting and frazzling would change that. I became patient, and the meaning of time shifted. I started to live in the moment.

I still travel solo. On the road, age has little meaning, and the generations mix into one friendly, curious, energetic mass.

Solo travel has empowered me in every sense. It has turned mountains into molehills and problems into solutions. It has been a time of lightness, few commitments, and many choices. It is perhaps the one thing I have done for myself, truly for myself. It may also be what has made the most lasting contribution and in large part turned me into what I am today: no longer fearful, but strong and capable. And filled with memories for a lifetime, as well as the yearning to do it all again, but this time with a cell phone.

21

Pick the Right Places, and Traveling Is Not Expensive

by Tim Leffel

Award-winning travel writer Tim Leffel is the author of four travel books. Part of this essay was excerpted from one of them: *Make Your Travel Dollars Worth a Fortune*. He is also editor of www.PerceptiveTravel.com, home to travel stories from wandering book authors.

How can you afford to travel so much?

Any person or couple who *does* travel a lot gets this question frequently. You'll hear it, too, when you're enjoying your retirement in exotic lands instead of watching TV or playing golf at home. A great number of travelers I meet in distant lands are not all that wealthy, however. Many are teachers, freelance writers, landscapers, or retirees who have to watch what they spend. They have more time than money, so how do they make it work?

It's simple, really: they go where their money is worth more than it is at home. Instead of spending a week in London, they spend a month in a place like Thailand, Ecuador, or Morocco.

In one issue of a travel magazine I looked at recently, the bill for a couple to have dinner at a restaurant near Angkor Wat — perhaps the world's greatest historic site — came to a total of $16, with drinks. One of the fanciest restaurants in Istanbul came with a dinner tab of $50 for two. At a comparable restaurant in Rome, the tab was $195 — for *lunch!*

If you're flexible about where you go, you can see much of the world for far less than you might expect.

After spending a few years traveling around the world, I published a book called *The World's Cheapest Destinations: 21 Countries Where Your Dollars Are Worth a Fortune.* It is now in its fourth edition. My main motivation for writing it was to show people that there are plenty of countries in the world where your own currency can really go a long way. You can still visit destinations where $1 will get you two pints of beer or a filling lunch. There are countries where $8 will get you a basic beach bungalow or an hour-long massage. There are places where $15–$20 will get you a car and driver for the day or a hotel with room service, a bellboy, and a pool.

We're programmed to think that travel has to be expensive, especially by the glossy travel magazines, when in fact it can be cheaper than staying home. Visiting great bargains doesn't mean settling for less. Some of the world's greatest attractions are in some of the world's cheapest countries. You can see the magnificent monuments you've read about since you were a child: the Taj Mahal, the Great Pyramids, Angkor Wat, and the fantastic structures of the Incas and Mayans. You can explore some of the deepest jungles, hike in the highest mountains, and view some of the most scenic vistas. You can visit a number of the best diving and snorkeling spots on the planet. You'll also encounter unique cultures and see architecture unlike any you've ever experienced. But this requires breaking out of the usual patterns.

If you like to drink wine, you've probably read an article at one time or another that compared very expensive wines with suitable substitutes. The idea is that while you may not be able to afford that perfect

$200 Bordeaux for your dinner party, there's probably a reasonably good other option out there for $15–$30 a bottle — or even less.

The same logic can also be applied to traveling to different parts of the world. Instead of going to expensive destinations in Western Europe, head east to Slovakia, Romania, Bulgaria, or Hungary. Or visit Buenos Aires, which has a European flair and sensibility. Instead of the expensive Caribbean honeymoon destinations, visit the islands and beaches of Honduras, Belize, Nicaragua, or Panama — even the Dominican Republic and Riviera Maya are a much better value.

If you have to be careful with your money and make it last through lots of golden years, then it makes sense to go where you can stretch your savings the most. Instead of Brazil, opt for Argentina, Peru, or Ecuador. Instead of Japan, Hong Kong, or Singapore, go almost anywhere else in Asia to chop two-thirds off your daily budget. Even in the U.S., substituting a small town or city for New York or San Francisco can slash your hotel or apartment-rental cost by half or more.

Let's go up a notch and look at meals for two in a

restaurant. If you travel to the Southeast Asian countries of Thailand, Cambodia, Laos, and Vietnam, you can almost always get a good local meal for a couple of dollars. You'll have to seek out pretty upscale places to spend more than $5 per person on lunch. On the other hand, you can easily pay $5 for one apple in Japan, and you'll be hard-pressed to even find a bowl of instant ramen noodles for that price at a Tokyo lunch counter. For what it costs to get one beer in Copenhagen, you can get a three-course lunch for two served to you in most of Latin America — with two beers to boot.

When it comes to hotels, prices between different countries can easily vary by a factor of two or three. For $40, about the price of a Motel 6® in the U.S.A., you'll be lucky to afford a private room of any kind in Western Europe, even at a hostel. In much of Latin America, that will get you a nice, big hotel room with character, right in the historic center. For that amount in much of Southeast Asia and the Indian subcontinent, you'll be able to book an air-conditioned room with daily maid service, a bellhop to carry your bags, and a nice pool.

Keep in mind, too, that even within a country, prices

vary by popularity and city size. Some parts are deluged with tourists, while others you can enjoy having almost all to yourself — with better rates. The Czech Republic is one of the most polarized examples: some 80 percent of the country's visitors spend every night in Prague. As a result, lodging prices in Prague are nearly as high as they are in Western Europe. Venture an hour away, however, and rates drop by 50 percent or more.

Mexico is a very large country, yet the top-five resort areas pull in nearly all of the foreign visitors. Go inland to the beautiful colonial cities, and you'll pay half as much for meals, taxis, and hotels. You can apply the same rule of thumb to many of the "greatest hits of travel": London, Paris, Rome/Florence, Barcelona, and Beijing. Sure, fly into those places and see the sights, but then venture outside them to the destinations where you can live it up in retirement instead of watching every pound, euro, or peso.

International travel doesn't have to be expensive. You can easily spend weeks or months overseas on a budget that's less than what you spend monthly at home doing nothing. The key is picking a spot where your money is worth a lot instead of a little.

22

Just a Backpack and a Rollie: Our Plan to Sell It All and Become World Travelers in Retirement

by Nancy Thompson

Nancy Thompson is an aspiring world traveler with a newly retired spouse. A late bloomer, she became a certified personal-fitness trainer at 58 and focused on helping mature women. At 60, she was inspired to create Flourish, building a community of women at midlife and beyond by producing a series of monthly salons and events to connect, inspire, and empower them. When Thompson and her husband hatched their plan to become citizens of the world in retirement, she knew they were not only going to survive but thrive. Today, she is a lifestyle blogger, sharing the adventures of retirement, shoestring travel, and living the good life wherever the road takes her. Her blog is www.justabackpackandarollie.com.

What is the appropriate response when your newly retired husband declares, "Let's sell everything on eBay and become citizens of the world. All we'll need is a backpack and a rollie"? To be honest, my first response was, "We *work* and can't afford to be world travelers. Exactly how will that be possible when we *don't* work?" Nothing like a cold dose of reality to put a quick end to his moment of craziness. Or so I thought. No such luck. "Backpack and rollie" became his new mantra. This man who had never really traveled suddenly wanted to see the world. Retirement can certainly shake things up.

Maybe he wore me down, or maybe he wasn't so crazy after all. I began to see that the backpack-and-rollie idea was a perfect metaphor for life as we approached retirement. What do we really need? It's all just "stuff" anyway. If we whittled it down to the bare essentials, could we fit a new lifestyle into a backpack and a rolling suitcase? Could two soon-to-be geezers who were newly retired, semi-adventurous, and on a limited income really become citizens of the world? Well, hang on, because we were about to find out. I became the self-appointed travel agent, tour guide, cheerleader, and guru of ways to travel on a shoestring. The

Internet became my new best friend. We spent many hours together, often long into the dark night. The glow of faraway places lit up the screen and fueled my imagination. I had become an armchair traveler, and I was hooked.

Adventures should not end when you retire. For many of us, that's when they really begin. Whether you have been a travel dreamer most of your life like me, or you're a new retiree who never had world travel on your bucket list, you can sign on for the adventure and say a wholehearted *yes!* to the opportunities that come your way. You never know where they might lead . . . but now you finally have the time to find out. Go for it.

It turns out that there are lots of interesting ways to travel for less or live the expat life for a while. What I've found is that living less like a tourist and more like a local only enhances the travel experience and greatly reduces the cost.

Imagine walking down 500-year-old cobblestone streets each morning, greeting every person you pass with a wave, a smile, and a *"buenos días."* Actually, I had been imagining just that scene for quite some time. Thanks to a very reasonable rental through the company VRBO®

(which stands for Vacation Rentals By Owner), we made it happen. We broke in our new travel shoes with a six-week stay in a home in San Miguel de Allende — a beautiful colonial town in central Mexico. San Miguel was the perfect place to "dip our toes in the water" of living like locals, and we dove right in.

Since I'm still working, I was able to hook up my laptop and magicJack and was quickly in business. Each morning, hubby set off to the *jardín* (town square) to sip a coffee, read the newspaper, and sit on a bench with the other retired gentlemen watching the world go by. Every afternoon, we set out together, mostly on foot, to explore our surroundings. I practiced my Spanish on shopkeepers, bus drivers, and any friendly person who stood still long enough. One evening we walked down to the *jardín* for a pastry and a coffee and found ourselves dancing through town with a group of about 50 revelers led by a brass band. *How?* you ask. Well, it looked like fun. We joined in. Turns out we had joined a prewedding party. We expected a quick trip around the square. Silly *gringos!* Traffic stopped. Not one horn blared, and on we marched. The best part? They handed out pottery cups and at every corner filled them up with margaritas. Back at the square we hugged the bride-to-be, wished her and the groom well, and strolled back to our house. We had tequila on our breath and huge grins on our faces.

If you look for adventure, you'll find it everywhere. I took Zumba® and yoga classes — in Spanish. We navigated the local bus system and only got lost once, agreeing to call it a sightseeing tour instead of the trip to the Mega Store that we had originally planned. We shopped at the *tianguis* — a weekly open-air market of stalls that sell everything from whole chickens to ladies' lingerie. I paid *cinco pesos* for two squares of toilet paper so I could use the public restroom. We walked in Christmas *posadas* (Advent celebrations), and every afternoon we bought tortillas — fresh, hot, and by the kilo. My personal favorite? Our 5:00 a.m. wake-up call every morning, courtesy of the rooftop rooster next door. I still miss that guy. We loved every minute of this adventure and are busy planning the next, and the one after that.

Traveling on a budget takes a little investigation and determination. I've become the research queen. I have the tiara to prove it. Some ideas are more adventurous than others, but all are worth a try. Our future travel plans include home exchange, house-sitting, and even exploring some of the new hostels that are catering to more adventurous senior travelers. Each offers the opportunity to travel short- or long-term, save a lot of money, enjoy the comforts of home, and really settle in and become part of a community.

Here's a quick overview of some resources for those of you who are looking to travel without breaking the bank:

Home exchange. If you own a home, there are hundreds of homeowners all over the world who want to swap houses with you. Some home exchangers also swap the use of a car and pet care. It's easy to sign up online on sites like Home Exchange (www.homeexchange.com) or HomeLink (www.HomeLink.org).

House-sit. Short- or long-term house-sitting opportunities are available worldwide. Retired singles and couples are in high demand as house-sitters. That's good news for us — we're experienced, we're reliable, and we probably won't throw all-night keg parties. House Carers (www.housecarers.com) and Trusted Sitters (www.trustedhousesitters.com) are great places to start.

Hostels. Many hostels today offer clean, private rooms, some with their own bathrooms, and a number of them even take online reservations (www.hostelworld.com). Currently, about 15 percent of hostelers are seniors, and that number is growing rapidly.

When my husband got caught in a corporate downsizing, he unexpectedly joined the ranks of the newly retired. We didn't see it coming and quite frankly were not prepared. Like so many others, we had been playing retirement catch-up and were hoping for a few more good income years. It knocked the wind right out of my sails, but my hubby is a guy who always sees the glass as half full, and he never missed a beat. His backpack-and-rollie idea sparked a whole new second act for us — one that's filled with opportunities for amazing travel adventures. See you on the road!

Section

LET'S GET AWAY FROM IT ALL

23

Glamping for Retirees

by Abby Jeffords

Abby Jeffords is a graduate of the M.B.A. program at the University of San Francisco, and is currently an account manager at Tag Worldwide and chief editor and partner of GlampingHub (http://glampinghub.com). Glamping Hub is a lodging-reservation platform that was born out of a business-entrepreneurship class and aims to bring travelers closer to nature by introducing the fresh idea of outdoor luxury and alternative accommodations in the wild corners of the globe. Jeffords manages the development of the company's creative content, with the sole purpose of helping to cultivate this new and exciting niche in the travel industry.

What is retirement, anyway? Is it a "gone fishing" sign? Is it an unabridged book of Sudoku puzzles? Is it a beachfront condo in Florida? Is it a Pulitzer Prize book list? Is it a thumbtacked map of the world? However we define retirement, there is one thing that every person should add to the top of his or her bucket list: glamping.

Glamping (aka glamorous camping) is not just for posh 30-somethings that want to enjoy the outdoors without getting their hands dirty. Pampering is pampering, and indulgence is indulgence, whether you are 35 or 65, and the stark beauty of nature is one thing on this planet that will never disappoint. The idea of outdoor accommodations may cause some anxiety among indoor types and less active travelers, and there are certainly some glamping sites that are more rugged than others. But the truth is that glamping makes the wilderness accessible to all, and for those who prefer superior comfort, chic design, and lavish amenities, there are a plethora of luxury camping sites that would rival the opulence of a four-star hotel.

Imagine this. It is nine o'clock in the morning. You are standing on a private deck in a sun-dappled wood on the edge of a quietly gurgling stream. All around you are tall, green trees with soft light shining down onto the leafy forest floor and the sound of birds chirping high in the canopy. Behind you is a large tent swathed in crisp, white canvas, the sides of which are pulled back like curtains to let the warm breeze flow through. Inside, the space is filled with intricately hand-carved wooden furniture, and a plush oriental rug covers the heated slate floor. A king-size bed stands in the center, fitted with plush, premium bedding and topped with freshly plumped pillows. In the corner, behind a decorative screen, is a full washroom, where a claw-foot tub waits, filled with steaming hot water dusted with rose petals. Clean, white towels are draped on the heated towel bar, and oversized terry-cloth robes hang on iron hooks. The whole room smells of jasmine and tea leaves.

Breakfast arrives on a large wooden tray laden with gourmet coffee, fresh fruit, and homemade breads. A bottle of Champagne is put on ice for later. The tray also bears a list of possible activities for the day, including fishing, hiking, horseback riding, bird watching, canoeing, and a class in nature photography. A picnic lunch will be delivered to you at noon, and a four-course dinner will be served in the main lodge at seven. After dinner, a bonfire will be lit in the center of the camp, and you and your tented neighbors can gather together, cozy up to the flames, sip from glasses of port or scotch, and gaze lazily at the infinite night sky until it is time to turn in.

You lean back into the deep seat of the Adirondack chair

on your sunny deck, sipping your coffee, enjoying the undisturbed beauty of the forest, and mull over a very serious and important question: *Why didn't I retire earlier?*

Glamping can be many things to many people: an escape from the bustle of everyday life, a family reunion, a weekend adventure getaway, a romantic rendezvous. For retirees, it can be any or all of those things, or it could simply be an opportunity to try something new and enjoy nature in comfort and style, either close to home, or in the far corners of the globe. Authentic safari tents, intimate yurts, soaring tree houses, and spacious teepees can all be transformed into luxurious, hotel-style accommodations by companies that specialize in turning your camping trip into glamping comfort. And depending on the location of the site and the nature of the surrounding landscape, the various daytime adventures can be arranged to suit any guest's desired level of activity.

You may be asking, "What if my 65-year-old pockets are not that deep?" Not to worry. Glamping is luxury camping, and can be defined in any number of ways; the one common denominator is that it will go beyond the basic level of pitching your own tent. As a result, there are glamping accommodations that will suit virtually any pocket depth: A snug, tented cabin in a sequoia forest, with two beds and a wood-burning stove inside, and a picnic table and barbeque outside. A thatched-roof bungalow on a pristine, tropical beach, with a communal washroom. A rustic yurt in the mountains, with a comfy queen-size bed and a full kitchen. For some, it may mean a DIY glamping experience. You may have to make your own bed in the morning, organize your own daily adventures, steep your own afternoon tea, and stoke your own fire at night, but there is one thing that will never change no matter how far down into your pockets you reach — the spectacular and constant beauty of nature.

So, ye of the golden years, put down that puzzle, close up the condo, roll up the map, and bookmark that novel. It's time to get up, get out, and discover luxury adventure in the wild.

Gone fishing? Nope. Gone glamping.

24

Look Local for Great Times

by Mike Bonacorsi

Mike Bonacorsi is a CERTIFIED FINANCIAL PLANNER™ and professional speaker, author, and radio-show host. He is the author of the book *Retirement Readiness*, and a contributing author to *65 Things to Do When You Retire*. His retirement tips can be heard nationally each night on *America Tonight*. He serves on the board of the Financial Planning Association of Northern New England as president in 2012 and pro-bono director. He is a member of the Souhegan Valley Chamber of Commerce and served as chairman for the expo committees. Bonacorsi is involved with several community organizations, serving as a board or committee member. In 2012, he was named "Volunteer of the Year" by the Souhegan Valley Chamber of Commerce.

E xperiential travel has been growing in popularity, and the opportunities are widespread. Imagine dogsledding across the top of the world, going on an African safari, biking through the French Alps, or hiking to a base camp on Mount Everest.

The allure of these vacations is to create or take part in the activities that will provide you with an "experience of a lifetime" that you can take home with you. It could be the adventure of a working dude ranch in Wyoming, the romance and luxury of travel on the Orient-Express, or becoming part of the local culture by volunteering in Ecuador.

Unfortunately, sometimes life gets in the way of our dreams, and just when we need that experience most, we find we can't get away. This can be a great time to look locally and take part in regional activities that can provide the same experience you're looking for, but with easier access and fewer restrictions.

During the summer of 2011, my wife, Karen, and I were looking for a few days away. Because time was limited, we didn't want to spend too much of it traveling — in order to get right into vacation mode, we decided to look locally. The coast is usually our go-to spot, but this time we wanted something different; yes, we were looking to relax, but we also hoped to find some activities to get our blood pumping.

After some online research looking close (within a couple of hours) to home, we found the perfect place and headed up to Lincoln, New Hampshire, in the White Mountains. Lincoln is a great spot to begin a vacation — it's a four-season playground offering skiing, hiking, golfing, kayaking, biking, fishing, you name it. Your visit can be as extreme or as soft as you want.

Our first day, we played golf at the Jack O'Lantern Resort (as usual, Karen won), and we followed that by going to see *The Full Monty* at the local playhouse (which, unfortunately, has since closed), and we roared with laughter through the entire performance.

After breakfast the next morning, we walked over to Alpine Adventures to get ready for a zip-line tour through the mountains. I have to admit that I was a bit nervous — it didn't seem like a big deal when we were initially planning this, but now that the time was near, it was a whole different story. The video loop on the wall didn't help matters by constantly reminding us of the height, distance, and speed we would be traveling while suspended in a harness from a cable.

The crew was friendly and reassuring as they reminded us about the great time we would have. They helped us into our harnesses, then checked and double-checked our setup and made any necessary adjustments. We piled into a bus and rode a few miles to a meeting point where an odd-looking, six-wheel, all-terrain vehicle took us to the top of a local mountain. All this time, I was looking around and thinking, *Am I the only one with butterflies in my stomach?* But as we got closer to our first zip-station, everyone suddenly got very quiet. I asked around and found out this was the first time that everyone else was zip-lining, too — and I wasn't the only one who was feeling nervous.

After a bone-jarring ride up a dirt path, we reached our destination. Crossing a short rope bridge, we crowded onto a platform constructed around a large tree on the side of an embankment. I immediately surveyed the area for any possible concerns; luckily, the platform was solid, the cable looked thick enough, and the crew appeared to be capable. Everything was ready to go, except me.

They called out for the first two pilots. I was considering hanging back a bit, when I saw Karen jump up to the front of the line, and without thinking, I followed. There were two runs at this station. "I'll race you!" she said. I glanced off the edge and followed the cable with my eyes — it extended a far distance and then seemed to disappear in the treetops.

The crew member checked our harnesses one more time and hooked us onto the cable. He counted off, "One, two, three, go!" and we were off. The fear and apprehension I had felt moments before dissipated as quickly as the wind rushing past me. Laughing and yelling to each other, Karen and I raced down the cable, with the rest of the group following us in the same way. I heard the rattle of the cable, then the voices of the others rose up, filled with excitement and delight.

Each run was a little different. The first and fifth were steep; the middle runs were longer. On most of them, we just stepped off of a platform, but one run required us to run down the embankment until the ground vanished beneath our feet. I overcame whatever fears I had and just literally got into the swing of the whole experience.

The conversation on the ride back was definitely different — instead of chattering anxiously, people exuded a sense of self-confidence as they spoke of their zip-line adventures.

The next day started sunny and bright as we rented bicycles, but a couple of hours into our ride we got caught in a downpour. Fortunately, we were close enough to a tourist center to run inside and wait out the storm.

The venue for dinner that evening was one that Karen and I had been discussing for several months: the Cafe Lafayette Dinner Train, one of approximately 20 moving dinner trains in North America. Operating since 1989 in North Woodstock, New Hampshire, the train consisted of three restored historic cars — the *Granite Eagle*, the *Algonquin*, and the *Indian Waters* — and offered travelers a 20-mile, 2-hour round-trip ride through the New Hampshire countryside, with views of the Pemigewasset River and the White Mountains.

Not knowing quite what to expect, we were excited to enter the train. The well-maintained cars brought back a bit of old-time elegance that usually escapes our casual modern world. But the real test would be the food — would we be served a high-quality dinner on this train trip? The answer was a resounding yes. From appetizers to dessert, we were not disappointed. Our waiter kept us entertained with stories of previous services and parties held on the train, and the slow, steady pace of the train was barely noticeable unless you looked out the window and saw the landscape drift by.

As the train pulled into the station for its final stop, we knew that the next day we'd be heading back to the real world. Yet, our local experiential vacation had worked, providing us with memories that would last long after we arrived back home.

25

A Great Gal-loping Getaway

by Jane Cassie

Since 1996, Jane Cassie's articles have appeared in more than 5,000 newspapers and magazines. As well as sharing travel stories with armchair adventurers, she loves escaping to her cottage in British Columbia's Cariboo region, where many more stories unfold. She is the co-owner and editor of Travel Writers' Tales (www.travelwriterstales.com), an active member of SATW and TMAC, and the past president of BCATW. To check out Jane and her husband/photographer, Brent Cassie, go to www.janecassie.com.

It's been a few years since I've straddled a saddle. And though my plump rump will likely survive the trot, I'm not so sure about the rest of my boomer-aged body. Do I still have enough core power to ride the range? Can I hang on tight when my steed picks up speed? My trepidation mounts (pardon the pun) as the herd of horses is corralled into the ring. With hoofs pounding and mud flying, they stampede through the gate and charge closer to the raised podium where I stand — or shake — in my boots. The only consolation is that the other two women who have joined me on this weekend retreat are shaking even more.

At different stages in our nursing careers — retired, preretired, and just plain tired — Sue, Carol, and I have come to Sun Mountain Lodge to revive, reconnect, and reclaim a little Western spirit. This getaway gem on the outskirts of Winthrop, Washington, promises all of the above and more. Like a diamond in the rough, it glitters from its mountaintop home and provides every nuance of comfort known to man- or womankind — posh accommodations, award-winning wine and cuisine, a pampering spa to soothe those saddle sores, and 30 head of horses to create them.

Beads of sweat drip from my brow as the galloping group invades my comfort zone. But, fortunately, help accompanies these well-behaved beasts. Kit Cramer could pose as the Horse Whisperer. Sporting chaps, spurs, and twin braids that fall from her wide-brimmed Stetson, she's a cowgirl to the core. Even her Western drawl sounds authentic. Thankfully, it also seems to mesmerize the energized pack, for in unison they obey her every command. In minutes, she has us perfectly pegged and paired with our equine companions. And before we know it, we're ready to giddyup and go!

"Each one of these 1,200 pounds of horsepower has a brain the size of a walnut," Kit chuckles, "but they all provide a safe four-wheel-drive ride." Her wrangling expertise is matched by a witty sense of humor, and while sauntering nose-to-tail along the rim of Sun Mountain's 3,000-foot-high plateau, I'm hoping there's truth to her reassuring words.

Nestled in a lush valley far below is Winthrop, a popular tourist haunt where we'd spent the previous day. We'd strolled the creaky boardwalks, checked out emporiums, and uncovered past and present treasures. As with most mining towns, the gold-rush boom in Winthrop was a colorful era. But once the resources dried up, so did the reasons to stay. We discovered that it wasn't revived again until 1972, after the completion of the North Cascade Highway. And thanks to the financial support from local lumber baron Kathryn Wagner, it took on a new Wild West flavor.

The elusive cowboy dream also lingers in the hearts of many who visit Sun Mountain Lodge. How can it not? Its 3,000 embracing acres are laced with enough trails, flower-choked meadows, and jaw-dropping vistas to satisfy any Roy Rogers wannabe.

"It's a great place to experience life as it used to be," Kit proudly says, as she guides us through a grove of trembling aspens. This is a gal who should know. Her family has lived in the Methow Valley for generations, and she has pretty much grown up on the backside of a horse. She's also coauthored Bound for the Methow, a coffee-table favorite that traces the region's colorful history.

We mosey along a trail just below the main lodge and find out it, too, has well-established roots. In 1965, visionary Jack Barron was so moved by this magnificent countryside, he wanted to share it with others. He chose this plot because it provided a 360-degree view of the mountains and valleys, and constructed his dream property out of local materials so it would blend in with the landscape. Three years later, the original Sun Mountain Lodge was open for business.

Although it's had major upgrades since those early days, the Northwest feel is still incorporated into this AAA four-diamond retreat. A total of 96 regionally inspired rooms are housed centrally, and any one of them, whether in the main lodge, or in the Gardner or Mt. Robinson buildings, would heighten our getaway. But on this trip, we decide to go for even more seclusion. We want to wine, dine, and enjoy our diva downtime without any interruptions. And our fully equipped home-style cabin at nearby Patterson Lake is certainly filling the bill.

From our promontory trail, we have a great view of this lake. A couple of canoes dot the glistening surface, and hugging up to one edge is a grassy shoreline that hosts our home away from home. Later, we'll catch up on lost zzz's, yak on our sun-splashed veranda, and sing along with John Denver. If we still have energy, we may even try another adventure. How 'bout fly-fishing, river rafting, or kayaking? Tennis or swimming, anyone? The courts and two pools sure look inviting. A hundred miles of hiking and biking trails also weave over this terrain. But for now, there's still more riding to do!

Later, we feel decadent as we dine in the lodge's restaurant. Accompanying Chef Bradshaw's artistically presented specialties is a wine list that would appease Henry VIII. With a 5,000-bottle cellar, it's not surprising to hear that the Washington State Wine Commission rated Sun Mountain as the top wine restaurant in 2010. And while we soak in the lush Methow Valley view and graze on goodies like wild antelope, diver scallops, and wild mushroom strudel, we naturally fill our glasses and raise them for one final toast. "Here's to revival, reconnection, and retirement — and, of course, one great gal-loping getaway."

Note: Although this year-round property offers the second-best cross-country ski-trail system in the United States, access to it via the Northern Cascade Highway is only possible from May to November.

Sun Mountain Lodge
P.O. Box 1000
Winthrop, WA 98862
Toll Free 1-800-572-0493 or 509-996-2211
Fax: 509-996-3133
E-mail: sunmtn@sunmountainlodge.com
Web site: www.sunmountainlodge.com

Section

VOLUNTOURISM

26

Voluntourism: A Growing Alternative-Travel Option Among Retirees

by Jim T. Miller

Jim T. Miller is the creator of Savvy Senior (www.savvysenior. org), a syndicated information column written for boomers and seniors that is published in more than 400 newspapers and magazines nationwide. Miller is also a contributor on NBC's *TODAY* show and on KFOR-TV in Oklahoma City, and is the author of *The Savvy Senior: The Ultimate Guide to Health, Family, and Finances for Senior Citizens* (Hyperion).

Nowadays, you don't need to join the Peace Corps to travel to exotic destinations and serve others. If you're looking to do more on your vacation than relax in the sun or go sightseeing, volunteer-service vacations — also known as voluntourism — are a great alternative and a growing trend among retirees. Today, many organizations offer short-term volunteer projects overseas and in the U.S., lasting anywhere from a few days to a few months.

Common program themes include teaching English, working with children and teens, building and repairing homes and schools, and assisting with community or environmental projects. In addition, volunteer vacations also give travelers the opportunity to experience the culture more fully and connect with the local people — much different than your run-of-the-mill sightseeing vacation.

Most volunteer-vacation groups accept singles, couples, and families, and you don't need to speak a foreign language. Costs typically range from around $700 to $1,500 a week, not including transportation to the country your site is in. Fees typically cover pretrip orientation information, room and board, on-site training, ground transportation once you get there, the services of a project leader, and a contribution to the local community that covers material and services related to the project. And, if the organization running your trip is a nonprofit, the cost of your trip, including airfare, is probably tax deductible.

Where to Look

While there are dozens of organizations that offer the opportunity to volunteer abroad, here are some good ones that attract a lot of retirees:

- Earthwatch Institute: A global nonprofit that offers one- and two-week expeditions that focus on environmental conservation and field-research projects all over the world.

- Globe Aware: Offers one-week volunteer vacations in 15 different countries.

- Global Volunteers: Offers a wide variety of two- and three-week service programs in 18 countries, including the U.S.

- Road Scholar: Formally known as Elderhostel, they offer a wide variety of volunteer-service programs both in the U.S. and abroad, usually to the 50-plus traveler.

- Habitat for Humanity: Offers a variety of house-building trips through its Global Village program and RV Care-A-Vanners program.

How to Choose

With so many different volunteer vacations to choose from, selecting one can be difficult. To help you decide, you need to think specifically about what you want. Ask yourself:

- Where do you want to go, and for how long?

- What types of work are you interested in doing?
- What kind of living situation and accommodations do you want? Do you want to volunteer alone or with a group? Do you want a rural or urban placement?

Once you know the volunteer vacation you'd like to go on, ask the organization for a description of their accommodations, fees, refund policy, and work schedule. Request a list of previous volunteers and contact them. Don't sign up with a group that won't supply you with this information.

If you're planning to volunteer abroad, find out if any vaccinations and/or preventative medications are recommended or required, by looking on the Centers for Disease Control and Prevention Web site. Also, check to see if your health insurer provides coverage outside the U.S. Many health policies (including Medicare) don't pay for medical expenses abroad. If you're not covered, you should consider purchasing a policy (see www.QuoteWright.com or www.InsureMyTrip.com) that includes emergency-evacuation coverage.

So, for all of you who are looking for travel opportunities that emphasize the joy of helping others, plan ahead and have a great time on your volunteer vacation!

27

Earthwatch Adventures

by Warren Stortroen

In 1996, two months after retiring from the Principal Financial Group of Des Moines, Iowa, Warren Stortroen was watching birds from a blind in Costa Rica's cloud forest. This was Stortroen's first Earthwatch expedition, and he was hooked. He has now participated in 73 of them, and he's already signed up for five more. He lives in St. Paul, and when he's home, he volunteers with the Minnesota Valley National Wildlife Refuge, Minnesota DNR Scientific & Natural Areas, and several related organizations.

As I watched from a makeshift observation blind and counted the duets sung by two male long-tailed manakins, a little green female manakin appeared on the perch about 20 feet away. She was immediately joined by the black-and-powder-blue males, who went into their noisy and acrobatic song-and-dance routine, courting the female. I had just retired, and this was my very first Earthwatch expedition — Dancing Birds — at the edge of the cloud forest near Monteverde, Costa Rica. Earthwatch Institute is an international volunteer organization that brings ordinary people together with prominent field scientists on research projects all around the world, designed to help ensure a sustainable future for our planet. The expeditions are ideal for retirees who are eager for adventure, who enjoy travel to exotic places, and who want to make a difference in the world!

On the Dancing Birds expedition, our six volunteers, from Japan and the U.S., spent two weeks working from a Quaker farmhouse on a study of the unique courtship ritual of this colorful little bird. There was cloud forest behind us, pasture in front, and a distant view of the scenic Gulf of Nicoya. The trees in the yard attracted a wide array of colorful birds, such as toucans and motmots. There was a modern bathroom and a kitchen to prepare our own breakfasts and lunches.

I enjoyed working with the dedicated volunteers and research scientists so much that I quickly signed up for my next expedition, which was an archaeological dig at an early Taíno site on Grand Turk Island in the Turks and Caicos. The volunteers learned to use a trowel, brush, and bucket while excavating 10 cm levels and keeping the walls straight! We learned to identify features and artifacts, measure the depth and location of the most important ones, and screen for the smaller ones. We found many pieces of pottery, shell, bone, and jewelry, and it was great fun working with the enthusiastic group of volunteers and scientists. On a later expedition, my most exciting find was a cloudy-amber fertility amulet — with both male and female features — from about 500 to 900 A.D. that I found in a dig site on the southern coast of Jamaica.

One of the most memorable expeditions was Mexican Megafauna. This was a search for bones of mammals from 1.5 to 5 million years ago, and specifically for those that crossed over from South America when the Panama land bridge opened. The site was an ancient lake bed north of San Miguel de Allende in central Mexico. The team spent two days at this site, where there was a lot of fossilized bone from ancient animals such as horses, rhinos, and mastodons. Then we moved to a new area in a maze of rugged arroyos to prospect for new bones that may have become exposed by erosion. I had my own GPS, so I made a home base and left the group to wander freely.

At an arroyo branch, I noticed a piece of mastodon tusk, and a little farther along I saw a ledge with some bone that looked like scutes (armor plate). I collected some and brought them to Oscar, the paleontologist, and he was elated. He said, "Warren! You've found a glyptodon! Can you bring me back there?" I had marked the GPS coordinates, so after lunch we returned to the area, where he spotted the carapace higher up in the arroyo. We spent the rest of the week excavating the animal, an ancient relative of the armadillo but the size of a small Volkswagen! It was about 3.6 million years old and probably the oldest and most complete specimen found in North America.

The red desert in South Australia was beautiful in the spring when I was there for Bringing Back the Bilbies. The research was on a 60-square-kilometer reserve near Roxby Downs, which was fenced to exclude rabbits, foxes, feral cats, and domestic grazers. Locally extinct animals, including the bilby (a nocturnal marsupial), the burrowing bettong (a small, somewhat vulnerable marsupial), and the greater stick-nest rat were then reintroduced with the hope that they could eventually be released outside the reserve.

One evening, volunteers from town joined the Earthwatch volunteers and staff for a census of the nocturnal animals. I settled into the warm red sand near my assigned bilby burrow as the sun was setting. Just as it turned dusk, a gray head with long ears and a long pink nose appeared! After surveying the area, the little marsupial hopped out, came towards me, and then bounded off into the swale to forage for grubs, beetles, and termites. He dashed right by another volunteer who was as thrilled to see him as I was. They are endangered and seldom seen in the wild except by dedicated researchers.

This is just a small sampling of the great adventures sponsored by Earthwatch. Retirees who are interested in reading firsthand accounts by volunteers can find articles on www.retirewow.com. Earthwatch Institute features expeditions in four general areas of research: oceans, ecosystems, cultural heritage, and climate change. The degree of difficulty of these offerings ranges from easy to strenuous. Accommodations vary — on some trips you'll bring your own tent and sleeping bag and share in cooking duties; on others, you'll stay in nice hotels with pools and all meals provided. These details are spelled out on the Web site www.earthwatch. org or in the briefing, so it's easy to pick the project that fits your needs and desires. I've participated in 73 expeditions across all categories and levels of difficulty, and I've truly enjoyed every single one. They are a great way to enrich your retirement!

28

Clem

by Ruth Clemmer

Ruth Clemmer has survived several careers: working as a law librarian; then in internal auditing for telephone companies, including AT&T; and finally at a wholly owned subsidiary of Xerox. After fully retiring in 2006, she traveled to Asia, Europe, Africa, Canada, South America, and the Middle East. She has taken part in expeditions at the Mammoth Site every year since 2007.

Road trip! Some people say Road Trip should be my middle name. Ever since the early 1970s, I've traveled all around the United States and parts of Canada by car. Before my retirement, I only had time for one road trip a year, but since my retirement in 2006 I generally do at least two and sometimes more each year. This year alone I have been to New England, Florida, and as far west as Wyoming.

Because of my penchant for veering off the beaten path, I have seen many interesting attractions over the years. By far, my favorite side trip was a lucky accident: in one of my stopovers, I found a brochure in the hotel lobby for the Mammoth Site in Hot Springs, South Dakota. The pictures were intriguing, so I knew where I was going to go next. When I left the hotel, I turned my car towards Hot Springs.

When I walked through the door of the site, the first thing I saw was a full-size skeleton of a mammoth! I paid my admittance fee and entered a whole new world. We walked up a ramp, around a corner, and there before me was a sinkhole. What made this different from any I had ever seen was that sticking out of the dirt were several mammoth skulls, many tusks, a pelvis, and lots of other bones I learned were all from mammoths. All of them were approximately 26,000 years old. Within the first five minutes, I wanted to get into the sinkhole and help excavate it. Imagine my surprise when I saw a sign that stated that if I wanted to help dig I should contact Earthwatch.org and sign up.

In 2007, I made my first excavation trip to the Mammoth Site. The first day, we were placed on a learning hill where we were taught the proper excavation techniques. After they determined that we were competent to begin real work, we were moved to a place that was thought to contain fragments or possibly a complete bone. Because this area was totally unexplored, you could make one scrape of your trowel and discover something amazing, or dig for days and not find anything except a few fragments. Even though I dug for two weeks and only found a couple of fragments, I couldn't wait to sign up for both two-week sessions the following year. I was hooked.

My second year, I dug for the full four weeks and found a few items: a toe bone, some pieces of ribs, and coprolite (animal dung). However, even better, I got to know two women who had also started their first excavation in 2007: Roberta O'Connor, a retired college professor from Florida, and Rebecca McCubbin, a retired teacher from New Jersey. We are all about the same age, have similar interests, and we meet up every year at the Mammoth Site.

When I arrived in 2009 I was given my assignment: working with another excavator, Ron, I was to prepare a tusk to be removed. This took us the first week, and on Friday the tusk was hoisted out of the bone bed. Afterwards, Dr. Agenbroad, the Director of the Mammoth Site, asked Ron and me to continue removing dirt from the large area where the tusk had been. At the end of the second week, Ron left and Rebecca replaced him. For the next two weeks, Becky and I continued to excavate the bone bed, finding only fragments and two pieces of rib. At one point, ground-penetrating radar was brought in to see if it could detect any trace of bones in several places. Nothing was found in our area of the bone bed, but Dr. Agenbroad wanted it to be excavated anyway, so we kept on digging.

On the last day of the dig, we came back from lunch and I scraped my trowel across the area where I had been working. I saw something different, but it didn't look like any bone I had seen before. I got out my dental picks and brush and began to slowly remove the dirt. What was this bone that seemed longer and wider the more I unearthed it? Just as my curiosity was growing stronger, I was told I had to pack everything up for the year. But I couldn't leave at this point. The next day, I asked Dr. Agenbroad if I could forgo a planned field trip and stay behind to continue working on my "find." He agreed, and by the time the others had returned from their field trip, I had uncovered enough bone to reveal that it was the ancient nuchal crest of a mammoth. This was the first skull found in eight years. Much to my delight, the skull has been named Clem after me.

I returned to the Mammoth Site in 2010 and began in earnest to excavate Clem; I discovered that a tusk found in 2003 was his. By now, his left-eye orbit and left tusk were uncovered. In 2011, right after I arrived at the site, a bone in my foot broke and my digging had to be limited. Olga Potapova, the woman in charge of the lab, set me up cleaning bones that had previously been removed from the bone bed. I really enjoyed that, almost as much as I do digging bones.

In March 2012, I returned to the Mammoth Site again to work for Olga for three weeks. The first bone she gave me to clean was part of a pelvis. While I was turning it, it broke. I was sure I was going to be sent home and told never to return. Olga could not have been nicer; she assured me that the bones do sometimes break. In July, I came back to continue excavating Clem. On the last day of the first two-week dig, I again asked if I could skip the field trip and just keep working on Clem. Before the group had left the parking lot, I became excited as I unearthed something truly momentous: *Clem's second tusk.* This brought the total number of tusks found in the sinkhole to 120, indicating that at least 60 mammoths have fallen victim to the sinkhole over the years. That July was filled with wonderful discoveries — my finds included two ribs, a toe bone, and part of a pelvis, all around Clem's skull. When you are digging and come across something, no matter if it is just a fragment or it turns into a recognizable bone, it is a thrill to know that you are the first person to see and touch this item in 26,000 years.

It's awe inspiring to think that a brochure in a hotel lobby could have such a profound effect on a person's life. Before I discovered the Mammoth Site, my goal was to visit at least one foreign country every year, plus go on one extended road trip. Well, those plans got turned around after I began my vacation excavations. This year, I made three trips to the Mammoth Site: two to work in the lab and one to unearth more of Clem's skull. I hope to eventually find his teeth so that we can determine how old he was when he fell into the sinkhole. Who knows what else I may discover? His whole body may be under the skull!

29

Somewhere in the World with Peter and Hinda

by Peter and Hinda Schnurman

Since 2000, Peter and Hinda Schnurman have been volunteering with NGOs in the developing world for several months each year, helping to empower people, organizations, and communities. When they are in the U.S.A., they support and volunteer with nonprofit organizations that also help people fulfill their potential. You can follow their travels and see their photographs at www.peterandhindas.blogspot.com and www.peterschnurman.com.

I n 1999, we decided to look for opportunities to spend some time giving back to society in a way we would enjoy, helping to teach and build the capacity of people who wanted to learn some of the skills we have. Since we love to travel, we began to search for volunteer opportunities in the developing world. At the time, we were fortunate to be working for two employers who would allow us to take a leave of absence to do this work.

For the next 12 years we volunteered each year for three to four months in different countries around the world. This created an opportunity for us to examine what we really wanted to do in retirement.

We are not good at sitting around. We are different in many ways, but after being together for almost 52 years we have grown to love and want many of the same things. Peter loves to volunteer and does it both at home and away. He is most happy when he is helping others to learn and to grow. He would like nothing better than to be able to travel most of the time volunteering. Hinda also enjoys volunteering, but has discovered that she needs to be closer to home for longer periods of time. One of our goals has always been to learn about other cultures and ways of life, and that has been fulfilled over and over. In fact, even though we feel we have given much — and we have — we have received much more in return, in terms of learning and understanding.

Peter is presently retired, and Hinda is still working part-time. We have volunteered in Thailand, India, Ghana, Namibia, Uganda, Kenya, and Ethiopia. Peter has been able to become conversational in the languages of all of the places where we have volunteered.

We have developed very close bonds and relationships with many people in all of these countries, and one of the pleasures of our daily life is to open our e-mail and to hear from friends from all over the world. How proud we are to have the honor given to us — not once, but three times — to name children of a family we have become very close to in a different country. It makes us nearly as proud as having one of our biological grandchildren named after one of us. Just a day or two ago I spoke by phone with my six-year-old Ugandan "grandson" and his Ugandan mother, my "daughter." He was so proud that he talked to his *muzungu jaja* — white grandfather — that he told his whole class.

Thanks to modern technology, we're able to stay in touch with people from organizations we've worked with, and we're even able to continue helping on some of the projects we first participated in years ago.

It has been our greatest honor to learn that some of the things we taught and tried to pass on are still being used by those we worked with around the world. So, in a way, we are still there — in Kenya, Uganda, Ethiopia, etc. For example, when we volunteered at an HIV clinic in Kampala, Uganda, we discovered that they had no medical-records system, so we helped them to develop a workable system that is still being used today. We also assisted in creating a distribution program for emergency food that eventually was used as a model by the World Food Program for all of Uganda.

In Kenya, we were asked to help raise money for a new building and then to help coordinate its construction. We began in 2008, and after making five volunteer trips there, we are happy to say that there are now two large and very modern buildings for which we provided technical training and construction-management skills. In one of the buildings, we helped to organize the first and only community-based dental clinic in the city of Kisumu, where a nongovernmental organization (NGO) that we volunteer for is located. This clinic has now become one of the most important and successful programs of this NGO. We are proud that the pharmacy in one of the buildings has been named the Schnurman Family Pharmacy.

We have learned to be modest in our goals and expectations. We know we can't change the world, but we've also learned that we can make small and important changes. We believe in the mantra that "if we save one person, we save the world." While volunteering in Kampala, Uganda, we met an 18-year-old woman who had been abandoned by her family and had gone to live as a servant with another family, where she was abused and became infected with the HIV virus. When we met her at the clinic where we were working, she was so weak that she couldn't lift her head to eat; she wanted to die. We visited her every day, accompanied by one of our coworkers, to encourage her to live. Slowly, she began to get better. We told her that she would get so well that she'd dance with Peter on his 70th birthday. We were overjoyed that this is just what happened when we returned to Kampala. In fact, she is now healthy and working.

In Ethiopia recently, we helped the NGO we were volunteering with learn how to reach out for new sources of support, and as a result of that, they are now partnering with the U.S.'s Centers for Disease Control and Save the Children, who are literally saving children who once were dying from malnutrition.

It is important to learn to look at the world from the point of view of where you are, not where you are from. We alter our ways to fit the place where we are volunteering, since not everything works in all places. Another mantra for us is to "do what you can in the place where you are, with the things you have, in the time that you have."

One of the best door openers for us wherever we go is to be able to converse, even a little, in the local language. People take it as a sign of respect for their culture, and that we are open to learning about them.

It is also important to be careful in today's world and to recognize that Americans abroad, especially in the developing world, can be "marks." In fact, between the two of us, we have been pickpocketed at least five times.

Our physical safety has never been an issue, but an important reason is that we always try to be careful. Our advice is: Be prudent. Don't take risks to prove anything, even to yourself. Also, you don't necessarily need to be afraid. We have lived in some very bad slums, but we know that being poor does not mean being bad.

Educate yourself as much as possible about the country you are going to. We start this process months before we actually leave. We learn about the organization we are going to be volunteering with, and the issues we are going to be dealing with. We try to hit the ground running as much as we can, because we are expected to accomplish a great deal in a relatively short amount of time. It's important to know that along with some great successes come many, many failures. We try to learn from each failure, and hopefully, the next time, the next place, there will be a success.

We do not view ourselves as being too good to do anything. We don't mind rolling up our sleeves and doing whatever it takes to get the job done. We try to be just Hinda and Peter. Most of all, we love what we do and we are always willing to learn from others, especially those we have been asked to teach. We deeply believe in making the world a better place for all people — no matter who or where. We know that anyone can learn, no matter what their education, religion, or background.

We have learned to understand and accept our own limitations and shortcomings. Living someplace other than one's own home, often in a very small space in less than optimal conditions (no indoor plumbing, no water from time to time, power blackouts, etc.), takes special effort for a couple. We usually work together and live together, and so we are with each other 24/7 for several months at a time. Our relationship with each other is strengthened each time we go away. And, we have become quite good at taking a sponge bath from a bucket, even in the dark, even when there is no power or water. What have we learned: keep candles and buckets of water handy.

We can look back over these past 12 years and feel a sense of accomplishment and pride. We are nearly 75 and 70 years of age, but we are already planning our next volunteer experience in Tanzania. We are not yet ready to stop. There is too much to do.

Visit us at our blog at www.peterandhindas.blogspot. com, and also www.peterschnurman.com. We would be happy to communicate with you if you are interested in volunteering to make our world a better place.

30

Change Your World!
Volunteer!

by Billy and Akaisha Kaderli

Billy and Akaisha Kaderli retired at the age of 38 more than two decades ago, and are now recognized retirement experts and internationally published authors on the topics of finance and world travel. They have been interviewed about retirement issues by *The Wall Street Journal*, *Kiplinger's Personal Finance Magazine*, the *Motley Fool Rule Your Retirement* newsletter, nationally syndicated radio talk-show host Clark Howard, Bankrate.com, *SmartMoney*, Minyanville, FOXBusiness, and countless newspapers and TV shows nationally and worldwide. With the wealth of information they share on their popular Web site, http://RetireEarlyLifestyle.com, they have been helping people achieve their own retirement dreams since 1991.

The World Needs You

Without the pressure of needing to bring home a paycheck, many retirees have chosen to utilize their expertise and newfound time in extraordinary ways. Around the globe, they are sharing what they know with those who are less fortunate.

For decades, Billy and I have been creating a meaningful retirement by getting involved with the local culture wherever we travel. It's a personal challenge, a perfect outlet for our creativity, and the rewards go far beyond monetary compensation. A couple of very special projects come quickly to mind — Billy's building of two additional tennis courts on federal land in a city park in Chapala, Mexico, and my teaching of Thai massage to willing, middle-aged students in that same fair city.

You Don't Have to Be Perfect

Let me paint the picture for you. Less than perfect, Billy's Spanish was what he could pick up from the streets and in cantinas. Grammar wasn't a priority, and his vocabulary was limited. As for me, I learn languages eagerly, but I usually do so in fits and starts. That was my approach when we first began volunteering in Chapala. Don't worry if it takes you a while to become really fluent — *the level of your language skills should not hold you back from volunteering abroad.* Communication happens in many ways. Just jump in. Everyone benefits.

You Are the Living Miracle in the Lives of Others

Billy had no construction experience. But that did

not suppress his enthusiasm. Researching online for instructions on how to best build the tennis courts, he printed out the plans. Then he collected about 100 loans of small amounts from individual expat tennis players, raising a total of tens of thousands of dollars. Today, these would be called microloans or peer-to-peer lending. Billy didn't have a word for what he was doing, but he knew it would work. With money in hand, he convinced the bigwigs at city hall in Chapala that the community needed this project, and he obtained their approval. With his ducks all in a row, he lined up the construction work with local talent, and the massive project began.

Living in the "land of *mañana*," he personally directed and supervised the five-week project, which then — of course — took two months to complete. A nearby abandoned building was turned into a "pro shop," and with the two new tennis courts, the total in the public park now came to six, qualifying it for serious tournament matches. Now, athletes from as far away as the capital city of Guadalajara came to play competitively, bringing their money with them. All those expat tennis players who donated cash for the cause were thrilled when, in just a few months, they were paid back in full. Today, classes for tennis lessons are packed with young boys and girls, introducing them to the sport, and this self-supporting tennis-court complex continues to be a source of local pride.

Share What You Know

After living in Asia off and on for almost a decade, I was fortunate to learn the art of Thai massage. Billy and I had the fanciful idea of teaching a shorter version of this massage method to some of the local Mexicans in Chapala on one of our visits. It was our hope that the Mexicans who learned this skill could supplement their household income, or offer massages in trade to their neighbors and friends.

Signs were posted around town, and word spread through the "taco telegraph" that free massage lessons were being offered two days a week at the Tennis Court Pro Shop! Men and women from all over the area signed up. I offered classes in two abbreviated versions of Thai massage: a half hour of head/shoulder/arm massage and a half hour of leg/foot massage. Both of these adaptations were safe and easy to learn, and could be done while the client was sitting in a chair.

The Best Was Yet to Come

Since classes were free, students would often bring

presents to me and my assistant as payment: fresh fruit from their gardens, edible gifts they made, or items from their personal stores. This was always a delightful surprise and showed how appreciative the students were for this opportunity to learn something useful. They also wanted to make it clear that, even though no fees were being charged for the classes, they were not receiving charity.

To create respect for this project, I required a hands-on exam to be taken by my students at the end of the course. After passing, their names were written on a "certificate of participation," along with my signature. This sort of official award of recognition is taken very seriously by villagers.

Months later, these men and women who were my students reported back to me that they were able to use massage techniques to ease the pain of family members. Some traded their services for extra cash, eggs, chickens, fruit, or other foodstuffs. At Christmastime, students delighted their families by providing massages to them in lieu of a purchased present. This saved them from spending money they didn't have, and the family was grateful for the massages. It also kept the students' skills fresh.

The bottom line? My students' personal self-worth was boosted by learning a new service that they could integrate into the fabric of their lives. My reward came in helping.

Meaningful Exchange

If you choose, retirement can be your time of meaningful exchange. Chances are that what you have to contribute will be highly valued by local communities worldwide. Hidden abilities or skills you possess as a dentist, teacher, artist, construction worker, doctor, gardener, musician, or companion are all needed right now in a community close to you or across the globe.

Find a need and fill it. Share the wealth of your personal talents with others. Your world will change, and so will the world of those whose lives you touch.

Section

FAMILY TIES

31

Important Conversations with Your Partner About Retirement Travel

by Dorian Mintzer, M.S.W., Ph.D.

Dorian Mintzer, M.S.W., Ph.D., board-certified coach, is a licensed psychologist, career/life transition coach, couples relationship coach, executive coach, consultant, teacher, and speaker. With over 40 years of clinical experience, she is a licensed third-age coach, a 2Young2Retire certified facilitator, and a licensed life-change artist. She facilitates workshops and speaks to community, corporate, and professional groups on topics related to midlife and second-half-of-life issues. Mintzer is the coauthor with Roberta Taylor of *The Couples Retirement Puzzle: The 10 Must-Have Conversations for Transitioning to the Second Half of Life*, which was published in April 2011. She is a contributing author to *65 Things to Do When You Retire*, *Remarkable and Real*, *Making Marriage a Success*, and *Live Smart after 50*. You can learn more about Mintzer at www.revolutionizeretirement.com.

Although many couples avoid discussions about retirement, most of them have experience with discussions about a different subject: planning a vacation. It's simple for many; one or the other makes a suggestion, the plans get made, and "off you go." For those couples, there may be a spoken or unspoken agreement about where to go and the "division of labor." In other couples, one person makes all of the plans, and does all of the work, and the partner comes along and benefits from the results. Occasionally, this works well, but sometimes the spouse who initiates the ideas and does all of the planning may grow resentful, especially if the other partner complains about the trip.

If deciding where, when, and how to travel is not so simple in your relationship, it doesn't necessarily mean you have a "bad relationship." It may reflect some difficulties in communication, decision making, and compromise. Since we're all influenced to some degree by the our experiences growing up, it's helpful to think back to how vacations were approached — and what it was like being on them — as you were growing up, and also when you were single. Share these experiences with your partner — it may help to clarify some of what you each want when you travel and why you view it the way you do.

The concept of retirement may change the way you look at travel. There may be some urgency; you or your partner may think, "If I don't go there or do this now, I may never get the opportunity again," because of age, health, etc. Some of this may be true as we age. Part of the challenge is assessing what dream is a "must do" and if — or how — the dream can be altered to accommodate changing health needs for one or both of you.

There are many travel options, even if there are discrepancies in your health and energy. Cruises, for example, offer something for everyone. There are also opportunities to travel for fun and adventure that may be combined with service work, learning programs, or intergenerational travel with children and grandchildren. There are endless possibilities.

It's helpful if you each develop your own "vision list" of things you want to do and/or places you want to visit. Then, find a time to talk and share your lists. Do they overlap? If not, would you be willing to visit those places that are important to your partner? Can you imagine enjoying the trip and not complaining every step of the way? I've heard many couples argue during trips and/or in the planning stage of deciding what to do. One of the worst experiences is to travel together and fight the entire time.

It's also helpful to open up to the possibility of traveling separately some of the time. Just like some couples decide to live separately during part of the year if one wants a warm climate and the other wants to stay nearer to the children or grandchildren, or to pursue other plans, the same might be a solution in terms of traveling.

The key is talking together, problem solving, and finding ways to compromise for the sake of the relationship. Jim and Brenda are a couple in their 70s, who've been married 50 years. Brenda has always enjoyed traveling more than Jim and retired a few years before him. When they traveled together, Jim would often grumble the entire time. She began to dislike traveling with him. They developed a compromise — she would go to Europe on her own or with a friend, and sometimes stay for a whole month. He would meet her there for a week, and they would then travel together. When he also retired, they decided to continue this arrangement since it was working. However, Jim recently admitted that he was getting bored with golf and fishing, and didn't particularly want to go back to Europe. Instead, he wanted to see different parts of the United States. On the advice of some friends, they decided to explore the northwest, since neither had been there. Although Brenda usually planned the trips, she asked Jim to "take it on." He took the task to heart, spent time doing research on the Internet, and planned a good trip for them.

Frank had always dreamed of buying a sailboat and traveling around the world. Betty didn't particularly like sailing, got seasick, and had no desire to sell their home and live on a boat. When Frank shared his dream with her, she nixed it, and stated that she wanted to go to Paris. Frank wasn't interested in that idea. They talked together and reached a compromise that worked for both of them. With the help of a financial planner, they realized that they could do two things: Frank could charter a boat with some friends and go sailing, and Betty could go to Paris with a friend. They each had a wonderful time and felt renewed when they were back together.

Here are a few tips to facilitate your travel discussion:

- Be sure that you talk with a financial advisor, so you know the realities of the timing of retirement and of travel.
- Set time to talk together without distractions.
- Use "I" statements.
- Share your own vision/dreams.
- Listen to your partner without interrupting and appreciate what you're hearing, even if you don't agree.
- Ask your partner why a particular dream is important to him or her.
- Try to view the discussion as an opportunity for a "win:win resolution."
- Try to open a space for the "we" of the relationship, so you can see what compromise is possible.
- Recognize that you can also have separate vacations.
- Try to add some time frames to your "shared vision."
- Be realistic: "We need to cut back on some expenses if we're going to be able to save for a trip."
- Be clear: "I have no desire to go to X, but I want YOU to go, so let's figure out a way to make it happen."

What's most important is to recognize that there is no "right way." What works in the first year or two of retirement may be different from what works down the road as life and health issues change. Talk, plan, anticipate, and be honest to yourself and your partner. Don't agree to something for the sake of agreement; instead, work to understand and appreciate your partner's viewpoint. The key is to honor yourself while at the same time finding ways to honor and nurture your relationship.

32

Maybe I Protest Too Much. Maybe Not.

by Samuel Jay Keyser

Samuel Jay Keyser, Special Assistant to the Chancellor at MIT, is professor emeritus in the Department of Linguistics and Philosophy. Aside from his career in theoretical linguistics, he plays trombone with the avant-garde Aardvark Jazz Orchestra and on a fire truck with a Dixieland ensemble, The New Liberty Jazz Band. A book about traveling with his wife, Nancy Kelly, entitled I Married a Travel Junkie, appeared in 2012, as did a memoir, Mens et Mania: The MIT Nobody Knows. His children's book, The Pond God and Other Stories, received a Lee Bennett Hopkins Honor Award for children's poetry in 2004.

The trick in retiring, everyone says, is not to retire *from* something, but *to* something. That didn't work for me, thanks to my wife. She lives to travel and now, unfortunately, so do I. Practically everyone I talk to about travel challenges me when I say I don't like it. How could I possibly follow my wife to 50 countries and keep a straight face when I profess that travel is not my cup of tea? They think I protest too much. I've been thinking about that.

When I look back on a particular trip, it is true that the low points fade into the background while the high points stand out. I remember the serenity of a Balinese temple and forget the towel-wringing humidity that made standing there unbearable. I remember looking into the eyes of a gorilla barely five feet away in the Bwindi Impenetrable Forest, and forget that the climb — up a mountain and through a thicket woven with nettles that tore at my clothes and my face — as we tried to find the gorilla was the hardest climb of my life.

In the recollection, the pain seems to have disappeared while the pleasure remains. It is a bit like childbirth, or so I am told. Maybe that is a built-in mechanism that operates in me, just as it operates in mothers who have told me they have forgotten the pain and remembered only the pleasure that came afterward. Maybe pleasure trumps pain. That would be nice.

In *Lyrical Ballads*, William Wordsworth defined poetry as "emotion recollected in tranquility." That definition will work for my relationship to travel. While I'm doing it, I find the effort stressful, threatening, and exhausting.

Once I'm home, I forget all that and remember the gorilla, the temple, the shrine, the garden, the people.

In this respect, I do think that I am different from the travelers I have known, and that I am not, in fact, protesting too much. The difference typically reveals itself over dinner after a day that has, for me, been filled with near misses, imagined terrors, and genuine sickness. Listening in, you might well think that my fellow travelers and I have much in common. A good deal of the dinnertime conversation is taken up with tales of mishaps: lost passports, sudden illnesses in the middle of nowhere, a spouse lost in a crowd with five minutes until the bus leaves, a reservation that was supposed to have been made but wasn't, a tour bus that was supposed to appear but didn't. The litany is endless.

In all of these conversations there is a fundamental difference between my companions and me. For me, the possibility of these misadventures is sufficient reason to stay home. But my companions recite these stories as if they were wearing rows of campaign ribbons across their chests. Like a war veteran, they point with pride to the red ribbon and reveal the story of the battle with a customs agent, or to the blue one and launch into the story of lost luggage turning up three days later with the locks broken. These are battlefield stories told by travel warriors eager to tell them. They can't wait for some other travel-veteran's story to be finished so they can begin theirs, in a sort of "you think you had it tough" exercise in one-upmanship.

There is a truth hidden in all this. For many of my companions, travel is a battle, a kind of ritual reliving of one's life compressed into a few weeks. Like a battle, travel is a test. They want to assure themselves that they can do it all over again if they have to, that they have not, in fact, lost it. Well, as someone who never had it in the first place, I say more power to them.

33

Travel to Rediscover Your Family Heritage

by Dave Bernard

Dave Bernard is the author of *Are You Just Existing and Calling It a Life?*, which offers guidelines to discover your personal passion and live a life of purpose. Not yet retired, Bernard has begun his due diligence to plan for a fulfilling retirement. With a focus on the nonfinancial aspects of retiring, he shares his discoveries and insights on his blog, *Retirement — Only the Beginning* (http://lovebeingretired.com).

The promise of travel once we reach retired life is easily one of the most universally anticipated and exciting rewards awaiting those lucky enough to survive the stressful working world. Who among us has not dreamed of escaping the everyday, so-predictable grind to visit some exotic, faraway place where our only duty is to enjoy the sunshine, lounge in peaceful surroundings, sample mouthwatering local foods, and subject ourselves to friendly folk whose only purpose seems to be making us happy? Some place away from it all where we have a chance to be ourselves, to do what we want to do, to enjoy rather than fret — that's the life! And now that we are retired, we finally have the time, so let the adventures begin.

As the newly liberated — otherwise known as retired — our venturing out usually begins with a journey here and an adventure there as we work through that list of places to go to that we have accumulated over a lifetime. For a while, we easily entertain ourselves merely by experiencing each new destination. But there is more to be had. Beyond the attraction of beautiful surroundings and wonderful weather, successful travelers — those who consistently get the most out of world wandering — look for something more, something deeper in their travel experience. For some, it may be researching the history of a place, to perhaps walk the same road that famous personalities of earlier days trod. Others get excited by learning all they can about the local people and their customs, or by taking in the natural wonders of the area, whether that means watching fascinating creatures slink through the bushes at night or plants bloom majestically with the morning sun. Whatever your particular cup of tea, your travel adventures can be enhanced if you are willing to spend the time to dig a little or have a personal interest in your destination.

If you really want to bring to life a travel adventure, try traveling in search of your family history. Most of us have a natural curiosity regarding our ancestors and the lives they lived across this country and around the world. What if you were to travel to places where your forefathers and foremothers were born and lived and loved? How about visiting the town where your grandparents built their first home? Or searching out the little church in the tiny village where they were married? Recent events can be equally inspiring, as perhaps you discover the spot where a particular dad nervously proposed marriage to a particular mom. Or where a favorite newly married aunt spent her honeymoon exploring the pyramids in Egypt for hidden treasure. Or how about tracking down the neighborhood ballpark where a playoff-winning home run was launched way back when? Your retirement travels will be that much more meaningful when the destination holds some personal significance.

Earlier this year, the Census Bureau released data from

the post-Depression era, making it publicly available for the first time in 72 years. Contained within were public records for 132 million Americans who participated in the 1940 census, including where they lived, what they did, and where they came from. This online data can be a treasure trove of useful specifics as you begin digging into your past.

To get started, make a list of interesting places where your family history evolved. Sit down with Mom and Dad over a nice dinner and bottle of vino and dig a bit. No one will be happier to share their past with an interested family member, and the memories they share can be incredible in their minute detail. Savor the experience as everything is recalled, from the smell of the jasmine in bloom to the sweltering heat of a particular summer day, from the exact name of that tiny village that rarely shows up on maps to what was eaten for lunch at a favorite café. During your discussions, specific moments and places that hold significance for the folks will surface, and there you have the beginnings for your plan of attack.

Look for pictures and albums saved over the years to find a photographic record of special places. It will be fun to compare them to the current state of affairs during your visit. School yearbooks will chronicle alma maters. Newspapers and magazines on microfilm at the local library can provide additional "before and after" shots of significant landmarks. The Internet offers a myriad of ways to gather relevant details. Any and all additional research will only add to the richness of the travel experience, providing a better understanding of how things really were "back in the day."

Recently, my dad gave me a copy of his side of our family tree. I was happily amazed to climb to the top and see the date of 1640, when our ancestors were fur trappers in Quebec! Something about knowing that our roots go back almost 400 years brings a quick smile to our faces and triggers our curiosity to learn more. Having been retired awhile and ever the travelers, Dad sold Mom on the idea of heading up north on a journey to visit some of the areas his forefathers populated. After a comfortable flight and a quick stop at the car-rental agency, they began a slow and tranquil journey through the local countryside that was once home to Dad's great-great-great grandfather. Over the course of some days, as they visited important landmarks such as schools and churches, town squares and old government buildings, historical landmarks and aged bridges, they began to develop a feeling for the area and the people who presently call it home. The two visited local graveyards in search of familiar family names and picnicked under shady trees beside slow-moving rivers. All along the way, the many quaint towns and shops with their friendly inhabitants added to the ambiance and enhanced the experience. Not only were they discovering new places, they were uncovering their past.

Visiting sites where your family roots began brings a deeper level of meaning and emotional significance to a trip. Learning details about where you came from and how your own family tree sprouted and grew helps you feel connected to all those who came before you. Experiencing the wondrous journey of your family heritage firsthand is only a drive or a flight away — and oh, what a wonderful trip it can be!

34

Retirement Travel — a Family Affair

by Dan Austin

Dan Austin is the founder and director of Austin-Lehman Adventures. Born in California, Austin first ignited his passion for adventure travel in the 1970s as a partner of a rafting company in the Pacific Northwest. His lust for travel soon took him to Alaska, where he saw opportunity as the owner of a construction company developing projects in a wide variety of locations, from remote Alaskan villages to military bases in Hawaii and the Azores. In 1994, seeking a new challenge, Austin and a partnership group bought Backcountry Tours of Bozeman, Montana. The purchase turned out to be the catalyst for things to come. In 2000, he partnered with retired industrialist and financier Paul Lehman, and Austin-Lehman Adventures was born. Along the path to owning and directing one of the world's most recognized active-travel brands, Austin founded the nonprofit Wheels of Change organization, dedicated to empowering rural Africans through mobility via donated bicycles. Visit the Austin-Lehman Adventures Web site: www.austinadventures.com.

W hen I was asked to share my thoughts, experiences, and ideas about what happens after retirement and how it relates to travel, the first thing I did was check with *Webster's Dictionary*! And boy, did they get it wrong: "Retire: to withdraw from office, business, or active life, usually because of age."

As I see it, we "retire" to travel! And for me personally, it goes even a bit deeper — we "retire" to *share* our love of travel. You see, the only thing better than travel itself is sharing the experience with others. For me, this started some 50 years ago. My first memories were of a cross-country family vacation in the back of — yes — the family station wagon. We spent the better part of four weeks crisscrossing the country looking for the world's largest ball of twine. We never found it, and I'm sure my sisters and I did not always get along . . . but there is no doubt that this experience made us all just a little closer, and it's stuck with me all these years.

Then, as a young adult, I started sharing my passion for more adventurous travel: first, I took a few friends and then small groups on weekend rafting trips throughout the Pacific Northwest. Little did I realize that this would be the foundation for a lifetime of travel, and that I'd eventually own and operate one of the leading adventure-travel companies in the world, Austin-Lehman Adventures.

While those early days were fun, exciting, and of course rewarding, it wasn't until I was able to share my love of adventure and travel with my own family — my wife, Carol, and my kids, Kasey and Andy — that I really understood how powerful this gift could be. During the summer, when Kasey and Andy were just on the threshold of attending public school, I'd pack up our bags and take the whole family on domestic adventures: deep-sea fishing for halibut in the frigid Pacific off the coast of Alaska, or a weekend excursion to Yellowstone, searching for bears and elk while hiking the endless forests of lodgepole pine.

Eventually, we grew to desire more exotic locations: six weeks in South America when the kids were 10 and 12 was a highlight, and a bike trip along the Mosel River in Germany when the kids were in their teens certainly opened their eyes to the opportunities that reside in the travel world. Those trips helped them grow to be the incredible young adults they are now;

while Andy is wrapping up his college degree, Kasey has now joined the family business, guiding our guests on tours and working in the office when not in the field . . . that passion for travel is obvious every day.

While life has gotten a bit more complicated, and all of us traveling together can be a bit of a challenge, that doesn't hold us back. We simply divide and conquer. Last spring, Andy and I were exploring the vast country of Namibia, photographing lions and rhinos up close and personal. Just a few weeks later, Carol and Kasey were off to Peru, hiking the lesser-known Salkantay Trek to Machu Picchu. We work diligently to plan at least one family trip a year, and we will continue doing so in the future as our kids have families of their own.

But wait, what does this all have to do with retiring and traveling? Well, it's really quite simple. As one of the leading tour operators in the world, we see all sorts of different guests. Our hands-down favorite programs are those driven by the growing segment known as multigenerational travelers. We are seeing extended families come back year after year to share adventures across the globe: grandparents, Mom and Dad, and the grandkids are all sharing a common passion for getting out and exploring this great big wonderful world of ours. What might start out as an experiment (grandparents suggesting that the family gets together for an adventure vacation) soon becomes a tradition.

It's amazing how it's not just the actual travel that brings the generations together — it's the planning beforehand that is fun for everyone as well. We have the benefit of getting in on the ground floor and helping facilitate this bonding experience. We advocate that everybody gets a say and is able to participate. It just makes the experience that much more powerful, inclusive, and lasting.

The stories and options are endless. Here are a few of my favorites:

There's that family of 21 (four families and Grandma) that travels every year on a trust fund set up by Grandpa before he passed away, to be used only for vacations. They alternate planning between families — nothing is off-limits — and all are obligated to join in. Sharing a week in Yellowstone with this group was an unforgettable experience, as we hiked the Wapiti Lake Trail to the colorful Grand Canyon of the Yellowstone, learned the differences between the four geothermal features of the Upper Geyser Basin, and splashed around in the Boiling River. They wrote to us afterward to say, "This was our best overall family trip. It is hard to accommodate the varying desires of our family [but] our guides succeeded!"

How about Grandpa and Grandma, who upon retiring set out each year to do something special with each of the grandkids, giving them lots of one-on-one time. Last year, it was taking the six-year-old twins to five national parks in six days by private jet. I can't wait to see what they cook up next. They told us, "There is no way we could have done this on our own, but with your support team, we were able to focus on that precious time with the grandkids and no stress!"

Three generations of one family joined us on our Vienna to Prague adventure. All had something "different" they wanted to see or do, including visiting the birthplace of the great-grandparents. From biking along the Danube River to paragliding over the Salzach Valley and taking a gentle canoe ride down the Vltava River, everyone found their perfect adventure memory. Their verdict: "We all had a blast."

You don't need to break the bank for an enjoyable

family vacation. We recently worked with three generations of a family to undertake their first-ever "camping" experience. We were so impressed with the energy and enthusiasm of these folks! Together, we created a custom Montana adventure that had them experiencing the best of the Big Sky while sleeping under canvas beneath a heaven full of stars. Heading off the beaten path into the Beartooth Mountains had everyone grinning from ear to ear. And that was even *before* we introduced them to s'mores! "It gave our family a chance to reconnect," they said appreciatively. You can't ask for better than that.

With a world full of great places to discover, there's no problem finding your own exciting adventure. When it comes to traveling in retirement, this could be a vacation that will bring you closer than ever to the people you most love.

35

Enrich Your Life: Travel in Search of Adventure

by Sam Dalton

Sam Dalton is the creator, executive producer, and host of *Boomer Adventures* (www.boomeradventures.tv), an Internet-based television program that takes baby boomers in search of adventurous places where they can share friendship, camaraderie, and fun. Dalton is also a respected national adventure-travel writer and contributor whose articles have been seen in magazine publications including *Family Fun*, *Backpacker*, *EcoTraveler*, *Touring America*, *Westways*, and *805 Living*.

When he is not on the trail in search of adventure, Dalton is also an accomplished actor and longtime member of the Screen Actors Guild-American Federation of Television and Radio Artists (SAG-AFTRA). His acting credits include roles in the original 1984 *Footloose* and on the NBC network daytime series *Santa Barbara*.

My youngest child was a toddler the first time he tagged along with his sister and brother and me on a weekend camping excursion.

It was a long-anticipated daddy-and-kids getaway that we hoped would be filled with a wide assortment of campside activities, and for which I thought I was well prepared. I wasn't. My youngest was still in diapers at the time, and diapers should have been included among the many family-dictated necessities I had carefully packed for our trip. They weren't.

In response to this inopportune occurrence, I improvised what might be considered a *unique* use for several of my well-worn undershirts. It was also the first time that I remember ever referring to such travel-related mishaps as just another one of life's great *adventures*. My now-grown kids still chuckle about that long-ago camping trip every time we reminisce about the many adventures we've shared. *And what memorable adventures they've been!*

We've rumbled about a majestic mountain range aboard an authentic wagon train. We've paddled furiously along rivers churned frothy by torrents of Class III rapids. We've drifted aloft in hot-air balloons. We've hiked; we've talked; we've shared indelible life-affirming adventures all along our way.

My kids have families of their own now, yet today I continue to forage about the world in search of adventure, whether I'm traveling alone or with my kids and their respective families in tow (when they have the time and inclination to accompany me). Even if they're not tagging along with me, my kids' familial penchant for finding adventure often permeates what comprises each of their own family's travel itineraries. I taught them well.

Yep. I am a baby boomer. Though I am loath to admit it, I have now reached an age that might be referred to as senior citizen by those inclined toward such pithy demographical labels. I'm not. Though my 60-something-year-old body occasionally belies the youthful physical condition I still believe it to be in, I manage to *get up and go* every day. My taste in travel rarely involves cruise ships, tour buses, and luxury high-rise hotels, not that there's anything that's particularly unattractive to me about patronizing any of them. For me, life is an adventure, and I'm fervent about exploring all the interesting places and things there are to see and do. Regardless of my destination, I either find or create adventure along every life-enriching step of my way.

You, too, can discover *adventure* anywhere, especially

when you guide your heart in its direction. Perhaps it is an inner longing for familial self-discovery that launches you on a mission in search of your genealogical roots. Or, it may be a historic small town that beckons to you, its weathered yet bucolic shops, restaurants, and Civil War cemeteries conveying a time when history once unfolded there in a tableau honed by war-earned glory and honor.

For me, adventure travel generally falls under one or more loosely defined categories: Archaeology, Art and Culture, Education, Escape, Genealogy, and History. Each has led to a cornucopia of experiences that have been thrilling, informational, relaxing, heart tugging, and even hilarious. Your list of categories may differ. That's okay. Regardless of what they are, make sure each provides you and perhaps your family with *adventures* that have the power to enrich.

I am blessed to have encountered countless such adventures — either on my own or with my kids — that have been memorable and life enriching. Here are a couple of special ones I have shared with my kids that will hopefully inspire you to go forth in search of your own wondrous exploits:

Dig it. Crow Canyon Archaeological Center (www. crowcanyon.org) seems to have been plopped in the middle of the Mesa Verde region of America's Southwest. Every August, this idyllic educational retreat reserves one week for families to come, learn, and perhaps dig alongside world-renowned archaeologists as they excavate ruins of the people who once inhabited the surrounding area — the ancestral Pueblo Indians (known as the Anasazi).

It was here one summer, amid those ruins, that I stood on the lip of a sandy cliff overlooking a canyon whose towering walls were painted ochre and purple by a setting sun. Across it, on the other side from me, danced my eldest son, silhouetted in blazing light. He had just unearthed a tiny shard of clay, and his voice echoed news of his discovery to me across the canyon's wide expanse. Later, an archaeologist who had been digging alongside him informed us that what my son had uncovered probably had once been part of a centuries-old Anasazi drinking cup. My son had dug up a *kitchen* relic from America's ancient past.

Drink up! While on assignment for my Web-based *Boomer Adventures* television program, my youngest son and I traveled to Beqa, one of 332 islands that comprise the tropical nation of Fiji (www.fijime.com). Beqa (pronounced "mbenga") is the island home of ancestral Sawau firewalkers, angelic church choirs, and laid-back resorts that drip with luxurious rustic charm. Inhale here, and the salty air is crisp and moist.

Roads on Beqa are nonexistent. So my son and I trekked along a trail that snaked its way through an emerald-hued jungle before depositing us at the edge of Raviravi, one of nine villages that inhabit the island. Across a grassy field that opened in front of us lay a contemporary two-story building with stucco walls and a tin roof. Inside, a village school-board meeting was about to convene, and the village parents, teachers, and school administrators who were in attendance invited me and my son to join them.

We sat cross-legged on the floor among them as they discussed items on the meeting's agenda, including fund-raising in order to buy outfits for the school's rugby team. Later, when an upturned baseball cap was passed around, my son and I gladly chipped in. Shortly thereafter, the school-board meeting adjourned and the real *adventure* we had hiked in search of began.

One of the men there brought in a bucket filled with water into which he massaged a sock filled with white powder. He was *brewing* up a batch of Yaqona, Fiji's muddy-tasting, tongue-numbing, national ceremonial drink. My son and I were the villagers' honored guests at that particular ceremony. Consequently, following the village chief, we were next in line to imbibe. My son and I exchanged knowing winks as we raised half coconut shells filled with the murky liquid to our lips for the first time and gulped it down.

B*ula*! Paradise.

Indulge whatever constitutes your idea of *adventure.* With our generation's average life span expected to carry many of us into our 80s and perhaps beyond, we who are baby boomers seem determined to embrace our so-called *golden years* with a zest for life equal in its fiery resonance to the passions that inflamed us when we were in our 20s. We've blazed all kinds of trails. Why not forge a few more adventurous paths that will open new worlds for you? After all, we went to the moon!

36

Travels with [Insert Your Pet's Name Here]

by Chris Kingsley

Chris Kingsley is the president and cofounder of Petswelcome. com. He lives in New Hamburg, New York, with his wife, two dogs, and a cat.

W hen I imagine my future retirement, I view it more as a continuum than a wholesale change from my current life. This is partly because, like many people my age, I will probably still need to earn a living. The change, then, will be in terms of priorities, spending much more time scheming and figuring out how to slip away whenever I can. This is a great pleasure in itself. But the real challenge, since it is, after all, my retirement, will be to get beyond the daydreaming and actually make it happen. And while I do have grand ambitions to go fly-fishing in

Patagonia and to follow the Tour de France around for three weeks in July, what I really want is what I've spent much of my professional career helping others do: I want to hit the road with my dogs.

Traveling with a pet used to be difficult. It took a lot of research and phone calling to find hotels or B&Bs that accept animals. And once you arrived, you were often treated like second-class citizens, charged a hefty fee, and relegated to the least desirable room. While these practices still exist, you can now find out about such places ahead of time on the Internet and avoid them. Even better, many hotels now actually cater to people who travel with pets. They have discovered that it's a growing market, and they offer not only quality lodging but amenities and services that are geared specifically for the needs of pet owners. Differing levels of pet-friendly services can be found at a wide variety of hotels, including smaller boutique chains like Kimpton Hotels, larger mid-priced lodgings like La Quinta, and even budget hotels such as Motel 6 and Red Roof Inn. It is not unusual now to find accommodations that supply treats, dog-walking areas, and pet-sitting services. Many concierges are even knowledgeable about local pet-friendly venues, parks, and events.

But finding pet-friendly lodging is just one aspect of traveling with a pet. The most important factor in deciding where you are going to take your pet is compatibility: making sure your pet's temperament and personality match your destination. It would not be a good idea, for example, to take your cat to a campground or state park where it could easily get lost or be harmed by wild animals. If your dog is high-strung and energetic, an urban environment might be too constricting and lead to unpleasant encounters with traffic, people, and/or other pets. It is essential that you know your pet's habits and idiosyncrasies, so that you can best gauge how they will react in specific circumstances.

Once you have taken this into consideration, the fun can begin. And the possibilities are endless. For example, you can plan your trip around your own specific interests. If you are a baseball fan, take your dog to one of the many Bark in the Park days offered by major and minor league teams around the country, including the New York Mets, Atlanta Braves, and Los Angeles Dodgers. If you like cross-country skiing and your dog(s) are hale and hearty, you can go *skijoring* (from the Norwegian, meaning "ski driving"), in which your dog pulls you on your skis using a special harness (for him, not for you). This popular activity is available in many states across the country, from New York to Oregon. Or you can even worship together at the Stephen Huneck Dog Chapel on Dog Mountain in Vermont. Depending on your location and the time available, you can make these short weekend trips or plan a larger vacation around one or more of your chosen destinations. Just do an Internet search for "[your interest] and dogs," and you'll be ready to head off on your next adventure.

Since the dogs I have owned have mostly been gun dogs or bird dogs — setters, pointers, and retrievers — that are bred for upland game-hunting, I try to take them to places with woods, fields, or beaches, so they can be in their element. Among the top pet-friendly national parks that include some or all of these topographies are Golden Gate National Recreation Area in California, Cape Hatteras National Seashore in North Carolina, White Sands National Monument in New Mexico, Padre Island National Seashore in Texas, Sleeping Bear Dunes National Lakeshore in Michigan, and the Big South Fork National River and Recreation Area in Tennessee and Kentucky. The national park system includes many more pet-friendly parks, equally diverse and worth visiting (and the state park systems offer even more choices). Again, with these sorts of trips, it is essential to know your dog's limits. Most pet-friendly parks require that you keep your dog on a six-foot leash, which is a very good regulation. While I plan on breaking a few rules when I'm retired, this is probably not one of them. Even though I feel confident in my dog's response, being in a new environment with many distractions might cause him to disregard my command, so it's better to be safe than sorry.

On the other end of the spectrum, there are many extremely pet friendly cities in the U.S. that provide a wonderful variety of fun and entertaining outlets for both humans and pets. Portland, Oregon, is one of the pet friendliest. You and your dog can literally smell the roses together (approximately 400 new types of hybrids) at Portland's Rose Garden, or stroll around the Portland Saturday Market in the Old Town District. Austin, Texas, is another dog-crazy city with their annual Dogtoberfest celebration. If you want to head down south with your pooch, Charleston, South Carolina, would be a very good stop. You can go on an Old Charleston Ghost Tour or explore the beautiful grounds of the Magnolia Plantation. Or, if you have a small dog, go on a sailing tour aboard a tall ship, Charleston's *Schooner Pride*. From New York City to San Francisco, you'll be able to find a wide array of animal-centric activities to enjoy in all our major cities.

No matter what you choose to do, taking your pet along will amplify and deepen your experiences, help make unfamiliar places more accessible, and add a delightful dose of unexpected adventure to your trip. Whether your retirement is an actual full-time affair or mostly a state of mind, it is still a wonderful opportunity for travel and discovery. I plan to use it as a time to acknowledge the daily pleasures that I've had little time for, ones that have been staring me in the face or, more specifically, nudging my butt and crying for me to finally get up, join them, and explore.

Section

UNUSUAL TRIPS

37

A Cartoon

by Mort Gerberg

Mort Gerberg is a cartoonist and author best known for his magazine cartoons in numerous publications, such as *The New Yorker*, *Playboy*, and *Publishers Weekly*.

He was voted Best Magazine Cartoonist of 2007 and 2008 by the international National Cartoonists Society. Gerberg also has drawn several syndicated newspaper comic strips and written, edited, and/or illustrated 40 books for adults and children.

Gerberg is the editor of *Last Laughs: Cartoons About Aging, Retirement . . . and the Great Beyond*, an original hardcover collection, and the author of *Cartooning: The Art and the Business*, the leading instructional/reference work in the field. Among his other popular books are the best-selling *More Spaghetti, I Say!* and *Joy in Mudville: The Big Book of Baseball Humor*.

"There go the Ewings, flying off again to some exotic locale."

38

Writing Workshops

by Elizabeth Berg

Elizabeth Berg is the author of many *New York Times* best-selling novels, two short-story collections, and two works of nonfiction. *Open House* was an Oprah's Book Club selection, and both *Durable Goods* and *Joy School* were selected as ALA Best Books of the Year. *Talk Before Sleep* was short-listed for an Abby Award, and *The Pull of the Moon* was adapted into a play. Berg's work has been published in 27 countries, and she is a popular speaker at venues around the country. She conducts writing workshops in the U.S. and in Italy. She divides her time between Chicago and San Francisco.

My writing workshops are designed to give women time and space to discover things about themselves both as writers and as human beings. I want to offer an opportunity for that rarest of things: reflection. Rumination. Rest. I want participants to take the time that they need to write something, think about it, revise it, and then go deeper. I want them to experience the value in having a room all their own away from their normal routine. During their stay, I want them to purposefully seek out beauty every day, either using my suggestions for certain places in whatever city we're in, and/or finding places on their own. Beauty mends and inspires. It bolsters up a sagging spirit. I want them to eavesdrop, to talk to strangers, to stand still and watch the way the wind moves the trees, to utilize all their senses in ways they might never have before. I want them to learn to trust their intuition — creatively and otherwise.

If you want to write most effectively, you need time to breathe, to look, listen, and feel. You need to understand that writing is immersion into an idea or ideas, and that it takes place both on and off the page — some of my best ideas come in the shower, or while dreaming. Quiet and solitude can help you do your best work, but the workshop will also provide you with the company of the teacher and the other participants twice a day. Our writing classroom is a safe and supportive place, and we try to check our egos at the door. A workshop is not a competition.

Writing-vacations.com came about because I took a cooking class in Italy that literally changed my life.

When the woman who ran the program asked me to come back and teach writing in combination with cooking classes, I readily agreed. Then, one night when we were sitting around drinking wine in Positano (as the sun set into the Tyrrhenian Sea), I said, "You know, Lauren, you should offer writing workshops for women that would let them be in beautiful places all over the world. Sort of a writing vacation." We decided that I would do another class in Italy, combined with cooking; and then do other classes stateside that just concentrated on writing. Lauren takes care of the paperwork, the welcome dinner, and welcome bag of gifts. I (and, soon, other award-winning authors) teach. My goal as a teacher is to inspire you to be the best writer that you can, and to be gratified and surprised by all that you find within yourself. I keep the workshops small, limited to eight, in order to give enough attention to participants. I insist that "my" women stay in nice places. This drives the price point up, but I also believe it helps contribute to a wonderful and productive experience.

For more details, please go to www.writing-vacations. com.

39

Wine Tourism

by George M. Taber

George M. Taber has written four books about wine. His latest are In Search of Bacchus: Wanderings in the Wonderful World of Wine Tourism and A Toast to Bargain Wines — How Innovators, Iconoclasts, and Winemaking Revolutionaries Are Changing the Way the World Drinks. Among his others, Judgment of Paris was awarded the 2006 wine book of the year by Britain's Decanter magazine. His second book, To Cork or Not To Cork, won the Jane Grigson Award from the International Association of Culinary Professionals, and was a finalist for both the James Beard Foundation Award for best book on wine and spirits and the André Simon Award for best wine book.

They don't make wine in ugly places. As a traveler looks around the world at wine destinations — from Napa Valley, California, to Bordeaux, France, and from Stellenbosch, South Africa, to Central Otago, New Zealand — it seems that one place is more exciting and beautiful than the next. Now that you are retired, you'll soon discover that there are an almost endless number of places to visit. The hardest thing is to figure out where to go first.

Wine country is often also food country. So you will probably be landing in a place where you can enjoy not only the exquisite wine but also scrumptious food. In most places, the vintners produce wines that go well with local food, and the chefs develop dishes that go well with the local wine. Those are marriages made in wine country.

I spent two years on the road working on the book *In Search of Bacchus: Wanderings in the Wonderful World of Wine Tourism*. If the publisher hadn't given me an advance to do the research, I should have paid him to let me do it. I visited 12 countries, and the toughest part of the assignment was deciding where to go. In France, Bordeaux is stunning, and the wines are among the best in the world. But how could you pass up Burgundy or Champagne or the Rhône Valley? My first introduction to wine and Europe was as a student in the Loire Valley. I used to ride a bike between vineyards. I never tire of going back to the Loire and recapturing the magic in a bottle.

With so many potential destinations out there, where do you start? For a first trip, I suggest that you stay close to home. Vintners now make wine in every state in the U.S. Yes, even in Alaska and Hawaii. It's not always great wine, and it is often made with grapes imported from California or Washington. But the products are usually interesting, and nearby trips are an easy introduction to wine tourism.

California, of course, is the Mecca of American viticulture and wine travel. A few decades ago, Napa Valley towered over every other region. There are now more than 400 wineries there, and you'd better bring your checkbook, because the price of everything from hotels to tasting rooms has become high. In recent years, though, other California areas such as Sonoma, Mendocino, and the Central Coast have come into their own. The movie *Sideways* takes place in Santa Barbara Wine Country. Some good wines are even coming out of Temecula, near the Mexican border. One big plus of these areas is that prices for wine, food, and lodging are much less expensive. Of course, only in the Napa Valley will you get a world-class restaurant such as the French Laundry in Yountville.

Oregon, Washington, and New York also offer good wines and good tourism. In addition, Virginia, Colorado, and New Jersey (yes, New Jersey) have recently developed fascinating wine trails, where you'll find beautiful scenery, fine food, and interesting wines. Some Virginia wineries, for example, make Norton, which seems to do well in that particular climate. Chrysalis Vineyards, outside Middleburg in Virginia, is one of the strongest advocates for Norton.

After a few trips around the United States, however, you really should stretch your ambitions and look abroad. The first challenge you are going to face is language. How comfortable are you wandering around in an area where you can't easily communicate with people? Some travelers love that; others hate it. I lived abroad for a decade in several European countries, so I've learned to get along in places with other languages. There is also the excitement of being abroad and experiencing new cultures. In recent years, I have visited wine regions in Georgia — the country, not the state — and in China, the next frontier of world wine. In each country, I hired a translator to travel with me. I had a wonderful experience in both places and learned about their wine cultures. But I would recommend those places only to the adventurous.

Once outside the U.S., a cautious wine traveler might

begin in countries where most people speak English. That would mean Australia, New Zealand, and South Africa. They are all long flights from the U.S. mainland, but worth it. They are wonderfully lively places where the scenery and the animals are great, and the wine is equally good. To be more specific, I'd suggest the Margaret River region on Australia's eastern coast, Central Otago on New Zealand's South Island, and Stellenbosch, South Africa. The racial scene in the last country is still a bit tense, but you can avoid problems by just being careful and smart. Some of my favorite stops in the three places I recommended above: in Margaret River, Leeuwin Estate and Vasse Felix; in Central Otago, Amisfield and Rippon Vineyard; and in Stellenbosch, Vergelegen and Fairview.

Perhaps my most memorable experience in wine tourism took place at the Singita Ebony Lodge in South Africa, where I went out to watch wild game every day at 5:30 a.m., 4:00 p.m., and late in the afternoon. In the days of Hemingway, the goal of hunters was to kill the Big Five: buffalo, elephant, leopard, lion, and rhinoceros. In this era of conservation, you shoot them with a digital camera. I bagged all five. Then at night, I would go into the open wine cellar and choose from among 200 of South Africa's best. My favorite was a 2000 Rust en Vrede Estate, a blend of Cabernet Sauvignon, Shiraz, and Merlot. Travel doesn't get better than that.

France, of course, remains the world's wine capital. I can never forget a sign I saw years ago on a fence outside a Bordeaux winery that read in French, "Visitors Not Welcome." That was pretty much the attitude of most people there at the time, but the French are wiser now. They are opening their winery doors, and it's now easy to find people, mostly young ones, who speak Oxford English. Spain offers better wine values than France, which can really cause a pain in the wallet. Italy has a combination of wine and culture in Tuscany that is hard to beat anyplace in the world. My favorite wineries for those countries: in Bordeaux, Château Lynch-Bages and Château Smith Haut Lafitte; in Tuscany, Banfi and Castello d'Albola; in Spain, Bodegas Dinastía Vivanco, which has the best wine museum in the world in addition to good wines, and López de Heredia.

There are as many ways to organize a wine tour as there are tourists. You can do it all yourself, if you feel knowledgeable about the area you're visiting. That is less expensive, but it can become complicated if you want to taste lots of wine and then drive back to the hotel. Most wine tourists in Napa do it on their own. In areas where you are not familiar, there are lots of tour companies. One day while at the Fattoria di Pietrafitta in Italy, I ran into two couples from New Jersey who were being driven around in a van by a local company called Wine Tours of Tuscany.

Your favorite wine stop, though, is going to be one that I haven't mentioned. It will be one that you just stumble upon for no particular reason. The winemaker will be delightful, and he will keep bringing out more bottles just when you are sure you can't handle another. That always happens, and it's why wine tourism remains one of life's great pleasures.

40

A Magical Cooking Experience on the Amalfi Coast

by Karen Herbst

In 1994, Karen Herbst decided to combine her travel experience with her lifelong passion for food and wine to create The International Kitchen. Herbst is recognized as one of the innovators of culinary travel, and, as an authority, is an adviser and frequent speaker to industry and professional groups. She is a member of the Board of Directors of the Italian Travel Promotional Council, as well as a member of the Slow Food Organization and the James Beard Foundation. In 2004, Karen was the honored recipient of the La Medaille d'Argent du Tourisme, the French Silver Medal of Tourism awarded by the French government. In 2008, The International Kitchen was given the coveted award of "Best Special Interest Product" by the French Government Tourist Office. Herbst is a member of Les Dames d'Escoffier, a worldwide philanthropic society of professional women leaders in the fields of food, fine beverage, and hospitality.

So, the time has finally come: you are retired. And also, the time has come to think about what you will do with your time, now that you do not have work commitments. And, maybe, it is time that you follow your dreams, act on a fantasy, do something you have always thought about doing. And, maybe, one of those fantasies has been to do a cooking vacation in Europe!

To call them cooking vacations is almost a misnomer. Sure, you do learn to cook the regional cuisine of the area of your choice, but this is really a cultural vacation. With roughly one week to spend at one of these programs, cooking and eating is the quickest and most surefire way to connect with the people, learn about their local culture, make friends, and come away with memories you will cherish forever.

But, these trips are not for everyone. You don't have to be a great cook, but you do have to have enthusiasm and a desire to learn. You also have to be willing to spend a week in the same location, no packing and unpacking, with excursions no more than an hour away. The groups are small, from four people to no more than ten or 12, depending on the location and size of the kitchen. In a week, there are four hands-on classes, so there has to be space for everyone to be able to easily participate in the preparation of the dishes. The classes are for half the day, then you eat the meal you have prepared, and the other half of the day is an excursion, often something food related, such as a cheese or olive-oil tasting, or a visit to a local winery. Also, there are visits to sites of historic interest in the area.

In addition, you have to be willing to be taken care of from the moment you are picked up at the designated airport or train station, and not to open your purse or wallet unless you choose to buy something. The trips include everything — transfers, accommodations, cooking classes, meals with local wine, excursions with transportation, visits, tastings, etc.

So, these are the "bones" of a trip. But it is so much more than that. People often come away saying that the experience has changed their lives. (I am not sure in what way, but we hear that a lot!) It is a time of relaxation yet enlightenment. This is a trip for anyone and everyone who is interested in opening themselves to a new experience. The cooking classes are an "equal opportunity" provider for all, bringing everyone together on equal footing — from CEOs of investment firms, to doctors, both medical and academic, to full-time homemakers, to people who never before did anything in the kitchen.

One of my great pleasures has been to accompany some of our special groups. In one, a woman was celebrating a milestone birthday and retirement, and she invited a group of her friends to join her and asked that I come as well. She asked for my recommendation, and I selected the Mediterranean Cooking Experience, a program we offer on the Amalfi Coast — it's one of my favorite places. The hotel is a small, boutique property of only 11 rooms. It is in a glorious location, on a hilltop facing the sea between the Bay of Naples and the Bay of Salerno, with lovely outdoor spaces, a vast fruit-and-vegetable garden, a beautiful pool, and a charming gazebo where all meals are taken al fresco whenever possible.

About ten years ago I met the property manager, and we decided to collaborate on a cooking program. With our immediate success, a fabulous teaching kitchen was built, complete with a wood-burning pizza-and-bread oven! During the cooking classes, we spend our time learning classic southern Italian recipes, sipping chilled Prosecco, and listening to opera. We laugh almost nonstop — this is indeed the best of times. There is no one who cannot succumb to the charm of all this.

After eating a leisurely meal of what we have prepared, accompanied by a wonderful local wine, we take time for an espresso before a bit of rest, and then it's off on an excursion.

One day, we are at Rosa's for the mozzarella-cheese demonstration. Another day, it is on to the famed towns of the Amalfi Coast — Positano, Ravello, and Amalfi. Each town has its own character and draw; if you absolutely must climb streets that are almost perpendicular, you will love Positano! Just be sure to crank up your treadmill to mountain-climbing mode to prepare ahead of time! And then there is the mystical isle of Capri. The adventure actually starts once you are in the small boat taking you to the island. If the weather permits, the boat stops so that you can swim in the sea, a truly sensual pleasure. You hit that cool, crystal-clear water, barely needing to move to stay afloat, and you are transported to paradise! Just watch out for the famed Italian mermaids, the *sirene*. . . .

But wait, there is more. You visit the remarkable ruins of Pompeii, and you stop to see how pasta is made in a local factory. Top this off with a dinner at a Michelin-star restaurant facing the sea. It is all almost too much to take in. . . .

There are places where you go that have such a magical quality that you cannot convey it in words; it requires the actual experience of being there. For me, this is such a place, and I feel the magic every time I am there. Indeed, not only magic, but healing. When my husband unexpectedly died four years ago, it was one of the few places where I felt comfortable going. It allowed me some tranquility and peace to begin the healing process. Yes, it is all here, relaxation and enlightenment — and enchantment, too.

41

Ranch Vacations

by Gene Kilgore

Gene Kilgore's name is synonymous with one of the world's great traditions. He has traveled thousands of miles exploring the world's ranches, bringing ranch country to millions of people worldwide. As a best-selling author, Kilgore has appeared on hundreds of radio programs and numerous TV networks, including CNN. He has also been featured in *The Wall Street Journal, People Magazine, National Geographic Traveler,* and *Sunset.* He is also one of the first lifetime members of the Dude Ranchers' Association.

R anch vacations began in the late 1800s, and since the very beginning they've offered guests from around the globe down-home hospitality, hearty food, camaraderie, and nature at its finest. Today, in the supercharged, technology-driven world in which we live, ranch vacations continue as a glimpse into the past, helping us all to reconnect with the natural rhythm of the Earth.

In ranch country, the sound of horses' hoofs, the howl

of a coyote, and the rushing of crystal-clear water off a mountaintop are the new sounds of rush hour. Here the air is pure, the skies blue as can be, and the folks who run these magnificent ranches serve up mouthwatering food and hospitality second to none. You can relax, kick back, and get back in touch with your senses, which have been numbed by high-tech gadgetry and the social-media frenzy.

Today, as in years gone by, baby boomers are discovering and rediscovering this wonderful way of life, a window into what was, and perhaps a look into the future to think about what really matters. For many 65ers, this is a time of change, along with exciting travel possibilities and opportunities to be with those who are most important in their lives. What better way to share precious moments with family than at a ranch where everyone has fun?

Some years back, I said on CNN, "Take your children to a beach and then, ten years later, ask them to name that beach, and they will have forgotten it. However, take them to a ranch, and they will remember the name of the ranch, the name of their horses, and maybe even the name of their wrangler for the rest of their lives." And that is really true. There is something magical about ranch country, especially for 65-year-olds. Perhaps it is the natural splendor or the chance to see kids and grandkids laughing, having fun, and playing the old-fashioned way. Remember those days not that long ago, when children could play outside and no one worried where they were or what they were doing? Well, in ranch country, kids can really be kids and grandparents can become heroes.

Today, there are ranches of all shapes and sizes, from rustic to five-star luxury, from thousand-acre spreads to smaller ranches surrounded by national forests. Ranches can be found in the United States, Canada, Mexico, Brazil, Argentina, and Australia. No matter which one you pick, you'll find the common thread is hospitality, followed by natural beauty, and in most cases an emphasis on horseback riding.

While riding is often the centerpiece of one's stay, ranches today offer much more than just that, and many more opportunities than when I began writing about them back in 1980.

What is really nifty about ranches today is that you don't even have to like horses or horseback riding to enjoy the experience. Some ranches offer fly-fishing, gourmet dining, tennis, swimming, white-water rafting, natural-history guides, massages, spa treatments, yoga, and more. Quite simply, what make these vacations so special are their wholesome and unforgettable adventures in nature. Everyone — the 65ers, the kids, the grandkids, singles, and families of all ages — can find a ranch to suit all wants and wishes. Ranches also offer facilities to professional groups, corporations, schools, and churches for seminars, retreats, and workshops.

Another really fun trend is to have a wedding at a favorite ranch — you might call these destination weddings, and of course a ranch can be one of the most exciting honeymoon spots in the world.

With so many ranches to choose from, it is hard to select one or two that are best for 65ers, but here are a few. Remember, so much depends on where you want to visit. For example, do you want to explore Canada? If so, check out Siwash Lake Ranch, an adults-only eco ranch in the heart of British Columbia. With 80,000 acres, this ranch guarantees plenty of riding and a romantic destination for couples. Or you may wish to head down to South America, where so many great ranch *estancias* are to be found. Los Potreros is one of my favorites. Run by two brothers who speak fluent

English, this *estancia* offers scenic riding and superb Argentinean cuisine. If you'd prefer to stay closer to home, try visiting one of the many ranches in the United States. On the eastern seaboard, check out North Carolina's Clear Creek Ranch, run by a couple who shares wonderful southern hospitality.

For pure luxury, head out West to Wyoming's The Lodge and Spa at Brush Creek Ranch, where pampering is just a way of life. For one of the best old-time ranches in the American West, visit Sweet Grass Ranch, a working cattle ranch where genuine traditions still thrive, in the heart of Montana. North, South, East, or West, wherever your travels take you, you will be greeted with a hearty welcome. To help you find your "home on the range," we created a one-stop Web site (www. RanchWeb.com) that shares information and advice on over 100 ranches, and even highlights what you might want to wear. This site brings the best of ranch country to the world, and we hope you will visit it often as you discover what I truly believe is the greatest vacation in the world.

I'm Gene Kilgore, and I wish you and yours safe travels and many more "happy trails."

42

Transformative Tanzania "Inventure"

by Margaret (Meg) Newhouse, Ph.D., CPCC

Margaret (Meg) Newhouse, Ph.D., CPCC (Certified Life Coach), has enjoyed five career-lets. She is currently focusing on writing and teaching about the second half of life, particularly sage-ing into elderhood and legacy, and she has a book in progress. She continues her active engagement with the Life Planning Network, a professional organization promoting life-planning for the "second half," which she founded and co-led for five years, and whose book, *Live Smart After 50!: The Experts' Guide to Life Planning in Uncertain Times*, she recently cocreated. She also makes time for her far-flung family (including grandchildren) and friends; music making; yoga, fitness, and nature; and learning and travel.

In early 2010, I was part of a 12-person group, selected by organizer/leader Richard Leider (www. richardleider.com), to spend nearly three weeks exploring Tanzania with David (Daudi) and Trude Peterson of Dorobo Safaris (reachable through their foundation, www.dorobofund.org). The trip was unique because it was an "inventure" as well as an adventure — that is, we took time for individual journaling and group reflections on who we are, what we want, and how this experience of "back to the rhythm" impacts us moving forward. We explored our surroundings with a multidisciplinary lens — anthropology, geography, zoology, psychology, political science — and we absorbed the deep ecological perspective of Dorobo Safaris, emphasizing the interconnections between land, animals, natural forces, and the inhabitants.

In our interactions with the indigenous Hadza and Akie, we experienced our ancient, gravely threatened preagricultural lifestyle, where egalitarian communities survive happily on what they can hunt and gather, possessing only their knowledge, skills, and absolute material necessities, such as knives, bows and arrows, axes, and cooking pots that they can carry with them as they move around.

Our group included three couples and six singles, ranging in age from their early 50s to 70. We bonded quickly and strongly, also with Daudi and Trude and our two Tanzanian guides, Simon and Charlie. We traveled lightly, camped comfortably but modestly, ate well and healthfully, and enjoyed excellent weather and unusually green surroundings. We shared deeply around the campfires and in the Land Rovers, laughed a lot, and made light of minor challenges — which, for me, consisted of being covered with insect bites.

Carefully crafted by Daudi and Richard, our itinerary included a mix of hiking and driving safari experiences, as well as meetings with various individuals and tribes. From the Serengeti and the Ngorogoro Conservation areas in the northwest, we moved southeast to the Yaida Valley and Tarangire National Park, then east through the Maasai Steppe to the Peterson family compound on the Indian Ocean. We encountered all manner of wildlife on foot (Daudi did carry a rifle), and we much appreciated the safety of the Land Rovers when a six-ton bull elephant in musth, frustrated by the "unreadiness" of his females, directed his surging testosterone at our vehicles (we tore out fast). There's no better way for me to evoke the experiences I had than to re-create a few of them for you, drawing you into a world both filled with adventure and mystery. . . .

Towering ancient boulders shelter our campfire and its puny but inviting circle of folding camp chairs.

Acacia trees cast lacy silhouettes against an indigo sky pierced with bright stars. The evening chatter of animals and birds provides a muted backdrop to our human voices. There are 12 of us "inventurers" on safari in Tanzania — 11 Americans and one Bruneian — and we listen raptly to the hunter-gatherer, Toroye, recount in matter-of-fact, graphic detail his very narrow escape, with a mangled butt, from a den of enraged lionesses several years before. When asked what a good day for him is, Toroye responds, "Meeting up with friends, discovering they are well and fed, and haven't been killed." Our guide, Daudi (David Peterson), the son of American missionaries who has spent most of his life in Tanzania, is Toroye's friend and the translator.

The next night we sit around the same campfire, after a meal of fire-roasted goat brought (alive!) by our guest Maanda, a striking, passionate Maasai woman in her 40s. We are mesmerized as she describes in excellent English the increasingly dire plight of the Maasai at the hands of corrupt central and district governments allocating their lands to the Arabs for hunting preserves. Her courage doubly impresses us, in light of a three-hour visit from the district police that very afternoon, designed to intimidate her.

A few nights later, in another camp, we are joined around the fire by a group of Hadza men and women, among the last hunter-gatherers in Africa. They describe their simple, self-sufficient life and the threat to their ancient culture posed by other tribes' grabbing their legally protected land for farming, with the government's blessing. Sometimes, they speak in their ancient "click" language, necessitating two translations; but spontaneous laughter, dancing, and singing bridge the cultural divide.

The next day, we clumsily follow the Hadza on hunting-and-gathering expeditions out in the bush. Our lean, agile guide, Endeko, gives up on elusive game and, following the directions of a "honeyguide" bird, finds two separate caches of honey. Oblivious to the stings of bees smoked out of their tree hives, he scoops out and passes around the larvae-laced honey while gorging himself. (Most of the second cache he carries back for his tribe.) I am beginning to grasp what an incredible storehouse of knowledge and skill these so-called primitive people possess. I can sense the thousands of generations who have gone before.

Three weeks of slow-paced, relatively carefree living

without a watch, computer, or telephone, amidst the wild animals and indigenous tribes, give me a visceral understanding of what "back to the rhythm" means. And I think to myself: I *want more!*

After I return home, I write:

The effect of the experience feels undramatic but profound, and the big question is whether I can actually implement my perennial resolve to simplify and slow down my life. I know I need more time outside in nature, more downtime, and less "stuff"; I hope my "No" muscles are up to this as effectively as my body muscles were to the hiking. In addition, I am:

- newly committed to conscious environmental protection and biodiversity;
- reconfirmed in the value I place on open-hearted community, so striking in Tanzania;
- freshly awed by the intricate interdependence and exquisite design of nature in all its diversity, from the Serengeti plains to the forests to the coral reefs. Nature is indeed "red in tooth and claw" but also full of wonderful niche sharing, as witnessed by browsers and grazers of different kinds of flora all peaceably coexisting, and symbiotic relationships such as the unattractive but essential "sanitary engineers" of the plains

— hyenas, vultures, dung beetles — or the honeyguides who lead the hunter-gatherers to the honey in return for the wax leavings;

- eager to spread the word about Daudi's passion and inspiring legacy, and to support the Dorobo Fund in their efforts to preserve the land and culture of the hunter-gatherers as well as the pastoralists (mainly Maasai).

Two-and-a-half years later, I wish I could say that my Tanzanian "inventure" has totally transformed me. But, honestly, it's a transformation in progress; a peak experience and touchstone for my ongoing attempts to simplify, slow down, savor my life, and act ecologically. I try to recapture that state of mind as I navigate an active "retirement." With gratitude to Daudi, Richard, and many others, I highly recommend what I would describe as a reflective and mind-stretching pilgrimage back to nature, community, and our human origins.

43

A Quest for Wonder: Machu Picchu

by Richard Bangs

Richard Bangs is the travel pioneer who cofounded Mountain Travel Sobek (www.mtsobek.com), was part of the founding executive team of Expedia.com, and has authored 19 books and produced many award-winning films. He is currently the executive producer and host of the Emmy Award–winning PBS series of specials *Richard Bangs' Quests* (www.richardbangs. com/Quests).

South America, with its many wonders, is a prime destination for retirees to visit. In order to experience all that is there today, we need to fly. And Lima, a short direct flight from major U.S. gateways, is the concourse for much of the continent. From here it's a quick hop along the rugged southern spine of the Andes to Cusco, gateway to a lost empire.

These are the Andes, the world's longest mountain chain, crowned by the highest peaks in the New World. The ancient capital of the Incas, Cusco nests at more than 11,000 feet above the sea. It's here I pick up the trail of wonder, and one of its key signposts, beauty.

Once the site of two colliding cultures, Cusco today is a striking blend of Incan and European sensibilities. Like most travelers who hail from sea level, I like to take it easy the first day in Cusco so my body can acclimatize to the altitude. Hotels, like La Casona Inkaterra, run by my old friend Jose Koechlin, greet guests with tea made from coca leaves, and it eases the entry into the high Andes.

Despite the rugged terrain and thin air, people have been living in the high Andes for over 5,000 years, building complex societies based on kings, gods, gold, and things of great splendor. The greatest of these people, the Incas, ascended to power in the 1400s, in part because of their brilliant engineering skills. The ability to build roads — 25,000 miles' worth — along with the fact that their domain was almost as vast as the Roman Empire, earned them the name "Romans of the New World."

Wonder is an offensive against the repetition of what we know. And the highlands of Peru brim with mysteries, magnificent things we don't understand, such as the Festival of Qoyllur Rit'i, which brings local peoples in their Sunday finery down from the high Andes to honor the Lord of the Star Snow.

And everyday life seems to go on, almost oblivious to the beauty that infuses it at places like the Sunday market at Pisac. Vendors, buyers, tourists . . . foods, fabrics, and faces — all elements of a living canvas still thriving in the Andes.

The Incas possessed a cultivated sense of aesthetics, interweaving the vivid and the graceful in their daily lives. And these aspects are alive and flourishing today.

That's not what the conquistadores had in mind when they set out to loot the treasure of the Incas. Beauty is in the eye of the beholder; where the Incas saw the tears of the sun in the gold they crafted, the Spanish saw only riches to be melted down for the cathedrals of Europe. Although the conquerors took nearly everything they coveted, beauty persisted. The Incas maintained their arts and crafts, traditions, music, and ceremonies, and perhaps most significantly, they managed to keep hidden a sacred citadel of thrilling grandeur.

The whereabouts of the Sacred City of the Incas was lost to lore, despite efforts of latter-day treasure hunters, historians, and archaeologists. But in 1911, an Ivy League–trained American named Hiram Bingham showed up in Peru, possessed with the idea of finding the lost city of the Incas. Some say he was the inspiration for Indiana Jones.

Jose and I set out as well, though in a fashion more comfortable than Bingham. We take the Inca Rail, which spirals into the valley like the shell of a nautilus. It's both like being in — and watching — a gallery of fine art, moving through halls of stunning landscapes and portraits, past period pieces and natural sculptures, back, back through time.

On the July morning when Bingham crested this rise, to his amazement he saw the ruins of an overgrown stone city perched on a narrow saddle. "The sight," he said, "held me spellbound. Literally, paralyzed as by enchantment, the spell of wonder."

Bingham called the place by its local name: Machu

Picchu, which means "ancient summit." Machu Picchu is a destination every traveler aspires to experience. Why? It may be because it is just so transcendentally glorious. This is the wonder of beauty.

Standing here, the world spreads out before me — the deep valley of the Urubamba River and the distant ridge of the Andes that encircle Machu Picchu. It's as if we're flying, with a condor's view of this riddle of a ruin. Temples, terraces, shrines, and sundials, all pieces of an exquisite puzzle.

Was this the royal retreat of the Incas, where the sumptuous artifacts and icons, and the wealth and wonder of the ancients were once hidden?

Or was it a religious site? The complex is dominated by sacred temples and shrines. . . .

Or perhaps there's an archaeo-astronomical explanation. Was Machu Picchu a giant observatory, tracking the sun's passage across the sky?

The Temple of the Sun was crafted in the traditional method — carved granite, no mortar — but with one striking difference: each block was angled back so that it would form a perfect crescent shape to surround the sacred stone within. Its two windows point to auspicious constellations and align with the summer solstice, so the sun's first rays strike the interior stone. Maybe we'll always have more questions than answers about Machu Picchu. But in the mystery there is a beauty that transcends the rabble of the senses.

When I ask Jose how this place affects those who come, he says, "People come here and they are awed by beauty; they are awed by what we're experiencing right now. We feel that there's something that moves us into just coming into yourself, some sort of introspection, those rare moments in modern life where you can actually get to be with yourself. How could you not be moved? There's something that people express when they go home; there's something that moves them."

Beauty is sometimes best when partially veiled, when it is an ambiguous, unfinished narrative. It fires us with wonder.

The Incas knew something we seek. When order combines with complexity, when elegance appears effortless, and there is a coherent but unspoken relationship among the parts, then there is enduring beauty.

44

A Gift

by Maeona (Mae) Mendelson, Ph.D.

Maeona (Mae) Mendelson, Ph.D., selected Morocco as the subject of her article because she was in the midst of cochairing the host committee for His Majesty King Mohammed VI Week in Hawaii. The occasion was the signing of the sister-state agreement between greater Rabat (the capital of Morocco) and Hawaii. In 2013, she begins an encore career as Director of the Intergenerational Center at Chaminade University in Honolulu, after serving six years as a volunteer board member of AARP and two years as chair of the AARP Foundation. Her favorite travel experiences are with her husband, family, and four grandchildren.

"B*alak, balak!"*

"Up against the wall, a donkey is coming."

Is there anyone who's written about Fes that hasn't described a confrontation with a heavily laden donkey? Edith Wharton commented on these donkey encounters in her 1920 travelogue *In Morocco.* These sensory ties to the medieval past draw the traveler to Fes, as do the crafts, music, and exquisite cuisine. Fes is one of the ancient cities included in numerous tours that traverse the countryside. These tours give visitors an opportunity to savor what is historically treasured, yet they may miss what makes Morocco dynamically contemporary.

Morocco draws the surfer, trekker, extreme-sports enthusiast, and food, art, and music connoisseur. Lovers of sumptuous destination resorts, shoppers, retirees on vacation, and expats will also feel at home. For all of them, it is a country vibrant with possibility.

My own sense of the possible in Morocco began in August 2001. I responded to an invitation to travel there to help plan the 2003 World Youth Congress. This event would bring 1,000 youths from over 100 nations to determine how young people could help achieve the United Nations Millennium Development Goals. With limited correspondence from my hosts, I boarded a plane in Honolulu, and some 28 hours later disembarked at the Mohammed V airport in Casablanca. I arrived without anyone's address or a telephone number. No one was outside customs when I passed through. With few alternatives, patience seemed my best option. In time, a university student spoke my name. I accompanied her as the sole passenger on a 40-seat bus to a college campus located on a multilane highway on the outskirts of Casablanca. Soon, I was joined by other international planners, who looked as bewildered as I was.

Every day, fast-moving trucks, cars, buses, and donkey carts sped nonstop by our dorm. Each day and night over the following week, my colleagues and I would bolt hand in hand across this broad expanse to the conference center. "You need a bridge or stoplight," I said during one of our planning meetings. When I returned in 2003 to attend the successful international congress, a stoplight had been installed. "Look," said my Moroccan friend, "it is your stoplight."

From this event, I began a decade-long relationship that has taken my friends, family, associates, and me to Morocco on numerous occasions and has brought old and new Moroccan friends to us. We call it our "rainbow bridge."

I am a curious but cautious traveler. In one of those psychological tests given to students, I would always select to read a book over going to a party, a hotel over camping. In other words, I never wanted to join the Peace Corps when it was offered in the '60s, and I don't think I would do it now. Yet, it was in Morocco that I changed my style of travel. I made a commitment to let go of my need to plan. I would be guided by what was offered at the moment. I have come to think of Morocco as a wellspring — a place to challenge my assumptions by asking, observing, and listening so that I can learn.

For example, in an unexpected visit to a nursery school in Rabat, I found an art room where children were seated in groups around large sheets of paper. A child handed me a paintbrush, made room in the group, and invited me to paint. I hesitated. "Please, please," he said. I started to paint, wondering when a child's ownership rights over a section of the paper would take precedence over sharing. I waited for the tears or the moment of confrontation. It never happened.

The preschool class was one of the quietest I had ever encountered. Since then, I have been invited to schools on a number of occasions where I have planted trees, watched plays, and helped with a dental-hygiene class.

It is odd. I don't volunteer in schools at home, although I've set up international mentor programs for children and older adults. This may be the ultimate magic of travel — it provides challenges we are willing to experience abroad but not at home.

What I find each time I return to Morocco is dynamic change. The country has had a strong economy in the past decade and responded to the Arab Spring with reforms within its Constitution. My interests are not political, and those youths and adults I count among my friends are the ones who work hardest for social change. Each time I return, the urban landscapes are different — new roads, bridges, hotels, and condos. What hasn't changed is the generosity of people I meet, the awesome beauty of natural landscapes, and a rich blend of Arab, Berber, Spanish, Jewish, and French cultures that goes back centuries.

To understand the contemporary is to be with people. It is the decision to have a conversation with a stranger on a train, to accept an invitation to a farmhouse, or to sip mint tea and eat pastries with college students in a café by the sea. It is sharing a lunch of fresh sardines and tomatoes with my sister on a beach in Essaouira.

I look for what is new — the fabrics, interior designs, jewelry, and clothing reminiscent of the ancient but on the leading edge in color and pattern. I enjoy the Gueliz in Marrakech and the Ville Nouvelle in Rabat as much as the *medina* (the old quarter of town). During the period of the French Protectorate, General Lyautey was smart enough to build the modern French towns outside the *medinas*, so that today the former grow exponentially and the latter have a visceral continuity to the past.

The Morocco that I experience today started with the serendipitous — a willingness to go beyond my initial level of comfort to enjoy and accept what has been given.

45

Seven Summits

by Carol Masheter, Ph.D.

At a time when many people's lives are slowing down, Dr. Carol Masheter's life has sped up. In her 60s, Dr. Masheter climbed the highest peak in each of the seven continents, becoming the oldest woman in the world to do so, according to the original Dick Bass list and the more recent Messner list. Dr. Masheter has been a research chemist, a university professor in human development and relationships, and an epidemiologist with the Utah Department of Health. She recently retired at age 65 to spend more time climbing, as well as writing and speaking about lessons learned in the mountains.

L ife is full of surprises. In my professions as a research chemist, university professor, and epidemiologist, I struggled with writer's block and fear of public speaking. I am afraid of heights. I would have never imagined that I would retire from a profession that I enjoyed to become a full-time mountaineer, author, and motivational speaker — at age 65.

A late bloomer, I had finally gotten my life together at age 50. I was a respected university professor and pioneer in a new line of research. I was in a long-term relationship with a man that I loved. Then my life fell apart. Within 18 months, I lost my job, my relationship ended badly, my mother died suddenly, and my only sister became critically ill. I could not sleep. My belly felt like demons were twisting my intestines into knots. I lost 15 pounds. Scared, I saw a doctor. He assured me that my symptoms were due to stress, not some terrible disease.

I decided to take a vacation from my troubles. I went to the Bolivian Andes for four weeks with a mountaineering-guide company. There, I learned to rock climb and ice climb. I also became adept at breaking big tasks into small, doable steps. I felt strong and fully alive in the mountains.

One mountaineering trip led to another. When I turned 60, the same age my father was when he died of his second heart attack, I got scared. Dad had taught me many useful things. However, over the years he had become inactive, overweight, and negative. In defiance of my own fears about becoming like my dad,

I climbed Aconcagua in Argentina, the highest peak in South America, in winds of 70 miles per hour. It was all I could do to keep from being blown off the mountain. I fought for each step. After nine hours of hard climbing, the thrill of reaching the summit reenergized me. Grasping the handmade cross that marks the summit, I threw back my head and howled with joy.

After Aconcagua, I decided to try Mount Everest. Though I was 61 and concerned that I might be too old to summit safely, I didn't want to die without knowing whether I could do it, simply because I hadn't made the effort.

To test a new training program to get myself in shape for Everest, I climbed Mount Kilimanjaro, the highest peak in Africa. Kilimanjaro felt like a walk in the park. The other client climbers were less experienced than I was, and this gave me an opportunity to encourage them, just as more experienced climbers had encouraged me when I started mountaineering.

Everest came next. It was a complex, rich, multifaceted experience with many challenges. When I stood on the world's highest summit, time stood still. Far below, neighboring peaks floated in a sea of fluffy clouds like enchanted islands. I expected to see angels floating by, playing harps and chanting prayers. It was the happiest day of my life.

On my flight home to Salt Lake City, I was tired, skinny, and quietly grateful to be coming back to familiar surroundings. After my plane landed, I hurried through the airport. A noisy crowd cheered and waved at the base of the stairs to the baggage-claim area with balloons, signs, and pom-poms. At first, I thought they were welcoming someone else, perhaps a returned LDS missionary. Then, I recognized the Executive Director of the Utah Department of Health, where I worked, as well as my colleagues, members of my outdoor club, my meditation group, my yoga class, a television news reporter, and a cameraman.

Happy chaos followed with hugs, congratulations, and an on-the-spot interview. The reporter's last question was, "What's next?" I mumbled something about finishing the Seven Summits, the highest peak in each continent, more to have something to say than from any true commitment to this goal. I was still getting my mind around the fact that I had summited Everest and had survived a harrowing descent while temporarily blinded from the altitude.

I thought I was done with climbing big mountains. However, within months, the urge to climb returned. Why *not* finish the Seven Summits? Other climbers I had met on previous climbs had described how beautiful they are.

My remaining climbs required more time than my allotted annual vacation from my position as an epidemiologist. A change in leadership at work prohibited me from taking further unpaid leave. I faced a difficult decision. I had to choose between work I enjoyed and finishing the Seven Summits. The loss of income and my professional identity was scary. Who would I be if I wasn't working? Nobody? Also, I was afraid I would run out of money and wind up poor, a bit nuts, and living under a bridge in my old age. I thought about it for several months. I decided a woman has to do what a woman has to do. I chose to retire in order to complete the Seven Summits.

At age 65 and 5 months, I summited Mount Kosciuszko, the highest peak in Australia, becoming the oldest woman in the world to summit all the peaks on the original Seven Summits list. Four months later, I trekked six days through thick jungle and knee-deep mud to summit Carstensz Pyramid, a fin of limestone in Papua Province, Indonesia, with an elevation of just over 16,000 feet, making me the oldest woman in the world to summit the more recent Messner list of the Seven Summits.

For me, mountaineering started as a break from the stress of a midlife meltdown. Climbing big mountains has led to over 60 invitations to speak to a wide variety of audiences, from first graders to graduate students, from prisoners to corporate lawyers. I have written a book, No Magic Helicopter: An Aging Amazon's Climb of Everest, which has been well received.

Mountaineering has helped me overcome my fear of heights, my fear of public speaking, and writer's block. As a retired person, I have a new identity and purpose. If, through writing and speaking about the lessons I learned from mountaineering, I can inspire even a few people to meet life's challenges, then I am happy.

Section

SPECIAL PLACES TO LIVE

46

Listening to Montana

by Donna L. Hull

"Flatlander to mountaineer" could be the title of Donna Hull's latest adventure. The boomer travel and lifestyle authority and her photographer husband, Alan, have recently relocated from Arizona to Montana's Bitterroot Valley for full-time living in "the most beautiful spot in the world." At Hull's popular Web site, My Itchy Travel Feet — The Baby Boomer's Guide to Travel, she encourages boomers to get up off the couch and go traveling. She's the boomer travel expert for My Well-being, powered by Humana.com, and the boomer travel columnist at MakeItMissoula.com. Hull is also the author of My Itchy Travel Feet: Breathtaking Adventure Vacation Ideas. Visit Hull at www.MyItchyTravelFeet.com and www.MyWell-Being.com.

In your travels, has a place ever spoken to you? When you arrived at a destination, did it feel as if you belonged in that very spot? Did your heart beat faster when a voice from somewhere deep inside you said, "This is my paradise"? That's what happened to me when my husband, Alan, drove our car down the driveway to Mystic Rose Cabin near Fishtail, Montana.

We'd been on a quest, driving all over Montana looking for a summer home. After 11 years of Tucson, Arizona's summer heat, our bodies yearned for the coolness of mountains and evergreen trees. From previous visits to the state, we knew that Big Sky Country had a hold on us. It was time to find out if the call was true.

Alan says my eyes lit up the moment we arrived at Mystic Rose Cabin. I bounded out of the car in a burst of energy to take in the view of the Beartooth Mountains. It wasn't the cabin itself, which is a modest log structure meant for vacationing and not at all like the home away from home that we discovered at Sweet Sage Guest House in Montana's Bitterroot Valley. So, why did I go all gaga over a simple log cabin that serves as shelter for hunters, fishermen, outdoor enthusiasts, and retirees looking for a relaxing getaway?

It was the view from the deck.

In the mornings, I'd sit on that wooden paradise, drinking a hot cup of coffee, my itchy travel feet propped on the railing. I'd watch deer grazing in the field to the accompaniment of water gurgling in West Rosebud River just down the hill. Beyond the deer's playground, rolls of baled hay were scattered across the land like pieces of a giant's chess game — some bales stood straight and tall, while others were tipped on their sides as if the giant had knocked them over in a fit of anger when he lost the game. Beyond the fields, majestic mountains touched the sky — the Beartooth Mountains. If I had the wherewithal to climb over the crest, I'd be gazing at the natural glory of Yellowstone National Park.

In the afternoons, I'd watch the drama of dark thunderclouds gathering across the mountains. Nature would put on an electrical show just for me. A lightning bolt would suddenly pierce the edge of an alpine peak, followed by a clap of thunder that reverberated throughout the valley. No longer considering the deck a paradise, I'd scurry inside to the safety of the sturdy log cabin.

Becoming One with the View

Alan and I took early-morning walks down empty dirt roads, waving to the occasional neighbor motoring by on his or her way to who knows where, or to campers turning onto West Rosebud Road for the 14-mile journey to the campground near Mystic Lake.

On rambling drives, we'd discover modest houses,

vacation cabins teetering on stilts near a river's edge, tractors raking strands of hay into giant rolls, and horses galloping across the thousand-acre ranch of some mighty mogul. On our way back to the cabin, we'd stop for dinner at off-the-beaten-path eateries like the Grizzly Bar and Restaurant in Roscoe or Montana Jack's, down the road from the cabin in Nye.

Civilization resides just six miles north of Mystic Rose Cabin at Fishtail, where a general store is the glue that holds the community together. You can find most anything in that store, from hunting supplies to local crafts to a surprisingly fine bottle of wine. Two buildings away, we'd order ham and eggs, pancakes on a separate plate, please, at the Cowboy Bar while eavesdropping on the conversations between the waitress and other patrons. Were they boomer retirees looking for a back-to-nature home, or third-generation ranchers scrambling to hold onto the land?

A View I Could Live With

Often, I'd sit on the deck of the Mystic Rose Cabin and say to myself: I could live here, if the winters weren't so rough, if Costco were closer, if Fishtail had a Chico's and a Starbucks — if, if, if.

I'd learn to ride a horse. I'd stand in the river, wearing waders, fly-fishing with the best of them. I'd hike into the Absaroka-Beartooth Wilderness to the jingling of bells tied onto my shoes to scare away the grizzlies; or, since wildlife authorities advise against the use of bells, perhaps I'd sing my way up the trail. I'd feel the cold spray on my face from a rafting trip down the Stillwater River. I'd stand outside on a cool summer night to view the Milky Way smeared across the dark sky, billions of stars making up that long, white blur that city dwellers never see. But, mostly, I'd sit on a deck with a killer view, tapping out stories on the laptop's keyboard about the land that holds such sway over this boomer writer.

Now I'm in the View

Ultimately, Alan and I couldn't resist Montana's call. We found our paradise on a hilltop in the foothills of the Sapphire Mountains overlooking the Bitterroot Valley on Montana's western border with Idaho. The weather's a bit kinder and gentler here than in Fishtail, and Costco, Chico's, and Starbucks are only 45 minutes away up Highway 93 in Missoula.

Now full-time residents, we have traded lazing by the

spa on warm winter afternoons in Arizona for snuggling by the fire on frigid Montana evenings. We whoop and holler at the sight of each snowflake and talk of snowshoeing, cross-country skiing, and snowmobiling.

Instead of the hustle and bustle of city life, we've discovered the slower pace of small-town living. Summer is filled with festivals and parades — lots of parades — and more hiking opportunities than we'll ever have time to do. And, always, there's the wave from a passing car or the friendly greeting from a townsperson that we don't even know.

Yes, there's a deck with a killer view where I sit in my favorite lounge chair tapping out stories on a laptop as the jagged peaks of the Bitterroot Mountains look on. Montana spoke to me. I listened and found my paradise. Have you?

47

The Journey Different

by Andrew Collins

Andrew Collins writes about travel and food for a mix of mainstream and LGBT publications. He's the editor-in-chief of *OutAloha* (about Hawaii) and *OutCity* (with a focus on Oregon, Washington, and British Columbia), and he's contributed to more than 170 guidebooks for Fodor's, including the recent New Mexico, Pacific Northwest, Arizona, Colorado, Florida, Caribbean, and Peru titles; he also developed and wrote the *Fodor's Gay Guide to the USA* series. In addition, Collins produces the Web site GayTravel.About.com, and has contributed to Orbitz.com, *Travel + Leisure*, *The Advocate*, and *New Mexico Magazine*. He teaches classes on travel writing, food writing, and freelancing for New York City's Gotham Writers' Workshop.

I opted for early retirement at age 23.

This — with tongue firmly in cheek — I've often told people, referring to my decision in 1993 to quit my job as an entry-level editor for Fodor's travel guidebooks and roam the world as an itinerant freelancer.

But over the years, I've come to see a certain degree

of truth in this statement. Retirement, after all, means different things to different people. Ultimately, I see it as the act of transitioning from one career or lifestyle path to another. And transition I did.

Although I permanently left the realm of conventional on-site employment, I continued to earn a living (I had to support myself somehow), all the while quenching my thirst for travel and adventure, and sharing my findings — through writing — with others. "Retiring" was the best decision I've ever made. In the unlikely event that one of these days I actually become financially secure, I don't expect I'll alter my approach to life. I'll still always be planning that next trip, and seeking an outlet for which to write about it.

Leaving my office job gave me geographical freedom. Since I couldn't afford to pay for a New York City apartment rental, I quickly discovered that I could work remotely. So, in effect, for the next six years I lived nowhere — which is to say, I lived all over.

I stowed my belongings in a storage locker, rented a post office box in my Connecticut hometown, and found overnight shelter in the homes of people whose pets I watched, as well as in the guest rooms of generous friends and relatives, the backseat of my car, and the beds of an almost comically varied range of commercial accommodations, from grimy, bare-bones motels in the shadows of interstate billboards to — occasionally — palatial, gilt-trimmed suites in regal, grande-dame hotels. I took on virtually every freelance project I could find, the most prominent and time-consuming being a guidebook I'd proposed, *Fodor's Gay Guide to the USA*, which came out in 1996. It was while researching this project that I visited the place that I'll forever regard as home: Santa Fe, New Mexico.

I put down roots in Santa Fe in 2000, ending my carefree spell as a vagabond (although to this day, I travel about half the time). I first visited New Mexico in 1994. It was love at first sight. After flying into Albuquerque one chilly late-March afternoon, I drove 60 miles north to Santa Fe, aptly nicknamed "The City Different." Indeed, everything from the earth-hued, angular adobe buildings to the fiery, chile-laced stews and enchiladas to the rarefied, piñon-scented air differed dramatically from anything I'd experienced growing up on the East Coast.

By that evening, as a vermillion sunset enveloped the

western sky, from the Rio Grande Valley to the jagged Jemez Mountains, I was hooked. I still remember calling my then boyfriend from a phone booth on Water Street, a block from Santa Fe's ancient cottonwood-shaded plaza, and declaring confidently, "I don't know when exactly, but I will live here."

I resided in Santa Fe (which has the distinction of being America's second-oldest city), and later Albuquerque, for seven marvelous years. And although I moved to Portland, Oregon — which I also love — in 2007, I return frequently to Santa Fe, always spending several days there. The rest of my time I head out on satisfyingly unstructured road trips around the region — through red-rock canyons in southern Utah, along erstwhile stretches of Route 66 in northern Arizona, in search of hot springs and ski runs in southern Colorado, and to everything from insular Hispanic mountain villages to wide-open mesas throughout New Mexico.

I've been to each U.S. state, including more than two-thirds of America's counties (my goal is to visit all 3,069 of them), and to every continent except for Antarctica. I will never stop wanting to visit new places. But it's to Santa Fe and the Four Corners region, where the snowcapped Rockies collide with the vast Chihuahuan, Sonoran, and Mojave deserts, that I return again and again, drawn to otherworldly landscapes that inspire and delight me every bit as much as they did on my first visit nearly two decades ago.

When I am asked to name ideal retirement destinations — to visit or to reside in — Santa Fe always tops my list. Much of my writing about travel over the years has appeared in publications geared toward the gay and lesbian community, and although I enthusiastically recommend Santa Fe to everybody, I do consider it especially appealing from an LGBT perspective.

It's a very personal choice, of course. Go elsewhere if you crave big and bustling urban centers, proximity to water, or warm winters (at 7,000 feet, Santa Fe is bathed in sunshine year-round but chilled by nighttime winter lows in the teens and 20s). It's a somewhat expensive, relatively small city of around 70,000, but if you're looking for a more affordable and still very gay-welcoming alternative, the much-larger Albuquerque is just an hour away.

Santa Fe's draws include a remarkably fertile arts and cultural scene: exceptional museums and galleries, several first-rate music and theater venues, a seemingly nonstop parade of vibrant festivals, and the renowned Santa Fe Opera. There's also much to please fans of the outdoors, from hiking and mountain biking to skiing and golfing. Northern New Mexico's rich indigenous and Hispanic heritage informs not only the arts perspective but also the region's distinctive cuisine, singular architecture, and warm embrace of diversity.

In a sense, and rather ironically, Santa Fe is both a post-gay destination, and a pregay one. It's had cachet with gays and lesbians for more than a century, well before resort towns like Key West, Provincetown, and Palm Springs became famous gay meccas. Today, although Santa Fe ranks second (behind only San Francisco) among U.S. cities in the percentage of households headed by same-sex partners, it's without obviously gay neighborhoods and has few gay-nightlife options. Local restaurants and bars, including the extremely fun, lesbian-owned Rouge Cat dance bar, cultivate a decidedly mixed crowd. As a "gay" destination, Santa Fe is extremely integrated.

There is one interesting gay subcommunity in Santa

Fe, however, and it's of particular interest to those of typical retirement age. Rainbow Vision, a residential village developed to attract LGBT folks in the "second 50 years" of their lives, opened here in 2006. The on-site restaurant, Garbo's, and bar, Starlight Lounge, have become popular LGBT social venues, not just among Rainbow Vision residents but with gay folks from all over northern New Mexico.

I don't know if I'll ever reside permanently in Santa Fe again. I find the concept of "home" every bit as slippery and malleable as I do "retirement." What I'm certain of is that for as long as I'm able, I'll continue planning trips to new lands — and I'll keep on returning to the place that most makes my heart stir, Santa Fe.

48

House-sitting as a Means to Travel

by Tracey Fieber

Tracey Fieber helps business owners simplify, automate, and grow their businesses and their lives. As the founder of Tracey Fieber Business Solutions, she draws on her more than 17 years in the financial industry in operations, marketing, training, and HR, as well as her experience as a personal and professional coach, to guide her clients to success.

In today's economy, plunking down money for travel expenses can be a luxury for those who are on a fixed income. Retirees on a budget who want to travel can do so as a house sitter. Caring for other people's homes in their absence offers you the opportunity to see the world without the expense and hassles associated with booking hotels and dining out in restaurants.

As a house sitter, an individual can live rent free in a

home anywhere an opening occurs. Besides keeping a watchful eye on the house, occasionally homeowners may ask the sitters to perform any number of tasks. A house sitter can take in the mail, care for a homeowner's pet, or keep the garden fresh. Some homeowners will even pay sitters in addition to allowing them to live in the home rent free, but typically this is just a straightforward swap.

The Benefits of Having a Professional House Sitter at Your Home

An unoccupied home is a target for vandalism. An occupied home is less likely to be targeted, so this gives homeowners peace of mind while they are away.

Sometimes, homeowners who have pets are looking for retirees to care for their cats or dogs while they're away on vacation. In this way, the pet's routines are not disturbed, and the homeowners have the assurance that someone is available to care for their animals as well as being a companion for them.

Many house-sitting opportunities are wide open in large cities such as Los Angeles, Chicago, and New York, where well-to-do homeowners often travel between more than one residence. So some house-sitting jobs can last for entire seasons, although the average sitting time is from one week to four months.

Experience May Not Be Required but Good References Are a Plus

House-sitting is ideal for retirees. It's not physically demanding. There is no need to take a class or pay for training to learn how to do it — and since many retirees are homeowners themselves, their experience alone gives them good credentials. Some homeowners may ask for references, but again, for a retiree, this is rarely an issue at all. It's important for both parties to sign a house-sitting contract that spells out specific details and instructions. Depending upon the location of the home, a car may not be required to get around, or one may be provided by the homeowner for the sitter's use.

If you own a pet and you're house-sitting, you may be able to have your animal companion house-sit too! Such an arrangement can be an ideal way to save on kennel fees, as well as allowing you to bring Fido along when you travel. In certain circumstances, the house sitter may have the opportunity to bring along a spouse and children.

Good house sitters, who are reliable and take care

of the home for which they are in charge, can obtain an excellent reputation. Many are called upon time and time again. As word travels that someone is a reputable house sitter, his or her business can become quite lucrative. For a retiree, this is an opportunity to supplement a fixed income if financial compensation is involved. And house-sitting can be an ideal way to take a vacation, particularly if the home boasts any number of resort-like amenities, such as a pool, a home theater, a sauna, a tennis court, an ocean view, or the use of a boat or a vehicle. A house sitter who has a proven track record will get his or her pick of desirable or popular neighborhoods.

How Can You Get the Word Out That You Want to House-sit?

Although you can begin by placing an ad in the newspaper in the area where you want to house-sit, there are Web sites devoted to matching house-sitters with homeowners. House Sitters America (www.housesittersamerica.com) is one such site where sitters pay a nominal annual fee to post an advertisement for U.S.-only locations. Homeowners pay nothing to use the site to locate sitters.

Other Web sites, such as MindMyHouse (www.mindmyhouse.com) are global and advertise in numerous countries, including the U.S.

Another option is to house-sit for homes that are for sale and unoccupied. ShowHomes (www.showhomes.com), which is a home-staging company, decorates the interior of a house and then hires a sitter (whom they refer to as a "home manager") to live in it while the residence is on the market. Homes that are occupied tend to sell faster than those that are empty. A home manager is responsible for turning on the lights, keeping the air conditioner running, sweeping up the leaves on the porch, and making sure the place looks clean and lived-in for prospective buyers.

So, if you are considering doing some traveling but don't quite have the funds for the trip, think about house-sitting. It's a great way to see the world without breaking the bank.

49

How to Travel Without Being a Tourist

by Teresa Roberts

Teresa Roberts is a reformed educator. After attending school for 49 years, either as a student or a teacher, she finally decided it was time to quit. Now an accidental author, digital nomad, freelance writer, and compulsive traveler, she has also founded the Web site Creative Paths to Freedom, where she explores the lifestyles of modern-day free spirits. She has written two books, *Finding the Gypsy in Me: Tales of an International House Sitter* and *Creative Paths to Freedom: How to Live Your Dream Life ASAP.* Living on the edge of who she is, while anticipating who she is becoming, is where she wants to be for as long as possible. She is a citizen of the world and a happy nomad.

Occasionally, I am mistaken for a tourist. Although I live in countries all over the world, I am not an expatriate either. Believe it or not, I am an international house sitter! Having chosen an unconventional lifestyle for myself, I am gloriously smug with my preferred style of travel.

Having an insatiable desire to explore this amazing planet, I retired about ten years earlier than most other people in my profession. Always a compulsive traveler, living abroad was naturally appealing. Yet, being endowed with a nomadic spirit, I was much too restless to move to a foreign location simply to sit down and become complacent in my new home away from home.

Since retirement, I have lived in Spain, Ireland, England, Prague, Malta, Mexico, the tiny island of Saba in the Dutch Antilles, and more. I even lived on a 57-foot boat in Baja, California. I take care of people's houses, boats, and estates while they are away. Often, I am there to look after beloved pets, but not always. Sometimes, I oversee other employees. Whether caring for greenhouses, gardens, pools, or even swabbing the deck, it is all good. I usually reside in each country for up to 90 days, the typical limit on my American passport, and no less than three weeks. Having the use of family cars, pools, the Internet, and all of the amenities of home is an additional perk. Some assignments may even come with a housekeeper, a gardener, tickets to the opera, or keys to the wine cellar. I have lived in a small brick bungalow with a view of the white-chalk cliffs of the English Channel and on a

1,700-foot cliff where I could see all of the islands of the Dutch Antilles while swimming in the pool.

I am not rich or well connected. Truly, I am just an ordinary gal who wanted to find a way to travel the world on a fixed income. In fact, I could be the poster girl for how to travel at any age on any income.

People become a tad confused when I disclose that although I am the proud owner of my own house-sitting business, I do not get paid for my services. Caring for the homes of others allows me to barter my way around the world. I have a monthly income of my own, so there is money for weekly groceries, public transportation, and occasional entertainment. Since I don't need to budget for hotels, car rentals, or expensive meals in restaurants, I save lots of money. For the price of a plane ticket, I can live in Malta for 90 days. That is cheap living! Yet, I don't live like a backpacking kid that has to wash her socks out in a shared bathroom sink in a youth hostel. I live in homes that are often quite extravagant, often nicer than my home back in the United States. Stocked larders and gorgeous patios in lush gardens where I can take my tea while enjoying the privacy and the comforts of home are all part of the exchange.

Imagine, if you will, a beautiful, little whitewashed village in Andalucía, Spain. I have passed many an idyllic day high in the Almijara Mountains in just such a place. Mornings begin with a perfect cup of Spanish coffee on my terrace while enjoying the breathtaking views of the Mediterranean Sea, more than 15 miles (25 kilometers) below. On a really clear day, the etchings of Morocco glimmer in the distance. Later, after siesta, I wander the narrow streets, savoring the cooler night air. I am intoxicated by the wild scent of Dama de Noche as it opens its blooms to a Moorish heritage. Sometimes, I end up at a bar or an outdoor restaurant, listening to the passionate sounds of flamenco music while sipping a local wine. Friends gather at my table, and we pass the night laughing, talking, and swapping stories.

A prime location like I just described is the single most important aspect that I seek in any new assignment. I find grand vistas to be inspiring, so outstanding natural beauty is something that I am not prepared to sacrifice. I know that if I'm committed to caring for a house, in contrast to being a tourist, I don't get to wander far afield when on assignment, so I need a "house with a view" to make it worth my while. Typically, tourists have a tight schedule as they run to and fro during a seven-to-ten-day break, with a country guide in one hand and a pile of luggage, memorabilia, and souvenirs tied to their ankles like a ball and chain. Their only free hand is used to wipe the sweat from their furrowed brows. That's not my idea of seeing the world! My quiet lifestyle requires very little of me, except that I be content to dally. I am a committed dallier. I dally a lot wherever I go. It is one of the single most beneficial perks of doing what I do.

Unlike a tourist, I shop in neighborhood grocery stores and buy vegetables and flowers from street vendors. I cook my own meals or find the places where local people eat. I walk a lot, but I am always home by the end of the day. Immersing myself in local culture and pastimes, I meet people who often become lifelong friends. Most important, my nomadic spirit is temporarily satisfied.

As I barter my way around the world, I love knowing that if I am drawn to another place, I'll eventually go there to live, too. Call me unconventional. I suppose that I am. Call me a happy retiree. I am deliriously happy. Just don't mistake me for a tourist. The world is my home.

Section

JOURNEYS OF
THE SPIRIT

50

The Road to Santiago

by Andrew McCarthy

Andrew McCarthy is an editor at large for *National Geographic Traveler*. His memoir, *The Longest Way Home*, released in 2012, was a *New York Times* best-seller. He is also an actor.

His name was Lars. He had wispy, unruly gray hair. Tall and lean, Lars stooped at the shoulder under his heavy backpack, and as he walked, he leaned far forward from the waist. This inclined posture added momentum to his already rapid pace, but it also made him look as though he might tumble over with every step. His long, thin arms swung as if without bones. His feet, already large, were made to appear even greater by heavy walking boots, while flamingo-thin legs protruded from khaki hiking shorts. As Lars propelled himself down the trail, his eyes squinted at the ground a few feet in front of him, as if scanning for a recently lost contact lens. I don't know how much of the northern Spanish landscape he saw with his gaze fixed on the dirt path immediately beyond his leather boots, but for nearly a week I walked in his shadow as we trudged toward the holy city of Santiago de Compostela.

Lars had been a high school teacher in a small Dutch village not far from Rotterdam, where he grew up. Each autumn for the past 30 years he had returned from the seaside, where he spent the summers, and taught mathematics. But this fall, in just a few weeks' time, he would not be going back to school. Lars had retired.

He was walking across Spain in order to come to terms with his decision to stop teaching. This was not something he told me in so many words, but rather an assumption I made given how he rambled on about the pros and cons of his decision. And as I was to discover about everyone making this trek, a deeply personal motivation lurked beneath the surface of every journey. For myself, I had glibly told friends that I was setting off to hike the ancient pilgrims' route because I was in need of "a good long walk" — but I was searching for a good deal more. I was a young man, just past 30, looking for a way out of an insular kind of life that had begun to not only confine me, but *define* me as well. My isolation wasn't in my best interest, and I knew it. Yet I didn't have any idea how I might alter my solitary habits. Then, after stumbling upon a book by a man who had chucked it all and changed his life by walking the width of Spain on something called the Camino de Santiago, I decided that a few weeks under the blistering Iberian summer sun was what I needed.

I flew to Barcelona, then made my way north, across the French border and to the tiny village of Saint-Jean-Pied-de-Port in the Pyrenees. With a feeling of dread and an overburdened backpack, I set out on a cool midsummer morning for an arduous haul over the mountains. After just three days hiking, I had to rest my blistered feet in Pamplona for nearly a week. But I trudged on, slogging from one village to the next, just like the hundreds of other pilgrims who plied the easily followed route. We were a ragtag global village, from across Europe and Asia and America, trudging toward Compostela. We slept in hostels, specially designed for pilgrims, called *refugios*. Alliances were formed and friendships made along the way. Except for me. I shuffled on alone day after day, trapped in my shell of isolation.

I first came upon Lars at the *refugio* in Frómista, a few days outside Burgos. He was surrounded by a small group, regaling them with a tale about a pack of wild dogs he had come upon and claimed to have repelled with his walking stick. I say "claimed" because, as I was to find out, Lars spun elaborate stories that were tethered to reality by only the most tenuous of strings. I hung on the fringes of the group while he waxed poetic, and I relaxed. Whether his story was true or not, it was well told and made me forget my own head games.

A few days later, I came upon Lars again at a small café during my lunch break after a particularly lonesome morning of walking. He was drinking coffee and butchering Spanish with gusto, talking to an ancient man who hung on his every word.

After finishing my meal, I walked on. Then, a few miles down the trail, as I sat in the shade of an expansive eucalyptus tree, I spied Lars lunging along the trail, his arms swinging like windmills, coming my way. He was alone. He stopped when he came upon me, and launched into a tale about the Knights Templar and how this very land we were crossing had played such an important role during the Crusades. I had no idea how much accuracy there was in this reworking of history, but for the rest of the day it kept me entertained as we walked.

And for a week it went on like this, me playing Sancho Panza to his Don Quixote — until the afternoon Lars sprained his ankle. As we sat in a café while he iced his foot, Lars insisted that I carry on without him, that I continue my trek toward Santiago. I hesitated to do so, but finally he wouldn't speak to me. He folded his arms and went mute across the table from me, unwilling to open his mouth. I thought perhaps he might begin holding his breath. Reluctantly, I relaced my boots and took my leave — the sight of him, steadfast in his silence, more upsetting to me than his swollen ankle. As I stepped back out into the light of day, I heard him call out for the waiter in his appalling Spanish, and as I stood on the street hoisting my pack, I could make out his high-pitched laugh.

Alone again, I walked on. But soon I made friends with a German woman, then a Canadian couple, then a group of Spaniards. The final two weeks of my walk were filled with fellowship and camaraderie. My time with Lars seemed to have released me from my isolation and planted me solidly into the center of the human race.

I saw him only once more — in Santiago de Compostela, at the end of the quest. Turning a corner outside the great cathedral, I saw a small crowd of people clustered around a seated figure. I edged my way closer and then heard the familiar high-pitched laugh. There, sitting on a stool, his foot propped up, was Lars, weaving another web before a rapt audience. I lingered for a few minutes, unseen by my friend, and when the group burst into peals of laughter, I slipped away — and never looked back.

51

The Sacred Side of France

by Colleen and J.T. Heater

Colleen and J.T. Heater have combined their interest in the lives of the saints and their love of travel to create a series of spiritual travel guides that lead to more meaningful and enriching experiences. *The Pilgrim's Italy* was the first in the series, followed by *The Pilgrim's France*. www.innertravelbooks.com

France, the number-one tourist destination in the world, features a wealth of art, fashion, gourmet food and wine, palaces, and the endless delights of Paris. Yet, just beneath the glitter is a deeper, spiritual side that is often overlooked. If, as a retiree, you're interested in more meaningful travel than the typical tourist fare, then a visit to the saints and shrines of France might just enrich your soul as well as your travels.

Our trip to France to research our second book on

This essay first appeared in *Catholic Life* magazine U.K. in 2008 and is reprinted with permission.

pilgrimage surprised us with a depth of spirit we did not expect. The French have a reputation for being more "in their heads" than "in their hearts," yet the Sisters and Brothers we met on our travels were filled with devotion, and the shrines emanated an unmistakable joy and grace. Admittedly, the numbers of religious staff at these sacred sites are small, but their prayers and piety could be tangibly felt.

As we delved into the pilgrimage routes of France, we found that sojourners of old set off to one of three destinations: Santiago de Compostela in Spain, Jerusalem in the Holy Land, and St. Peter's in Rome, Italy. These ancient routes crisscrossed the country, and cities were literally put on the map by spiritual seekers and their quests. Modern-day pilgrims are now visiting places where the Virgin Mary appeared over the last few centuries. The most famous of these is Lourdes in southern France. Lesser known but also popular is the Chapel of Our Lady of the Miraculous Medal in Paris, where our journey started. Across the street from Bon Marché, one of the premier shopping spots on the Left Bank, we made our way through a small arched entry off rue du Bac. This is where St. Catherine Labouré was visited three times by the

Virgin Mary in 1830, and where Mary asked that a special medal be made in her honor.

Finding the Chapel of the Miraculous Medal and an upscale department store in the same location initially struck us as odd, but when we witnessed many Parisians dropping in for mass and prayer it became clear that the shrine served as an oasis of peace amidst the retail frenzy of Paris. Though always active, the chapel is a place of deep devotion and attracts pilgrimage groups from around the world. Two saints, Catherine Labouré and Louise de Marillac, are enshrined here, as is the heart of St. Vincent de Paul. Meditating with other prayerful souls, we felt inwardly blessed and our spirits uplifted — a markedly different kind of experience from shopping at Bon Marché!

Within a two-block radius we visited another pair of shrines: the Chapel of St. Vincent de Paul on rue de Sèvres, and the Society of Foreign Missions on rue du Bac, with its peaceful chapel and crypt. After buying a gourmet picnic lunch from the beautiful food market at La Grande Épicerie de Paris, located between these two locations, we ate with the locals in the walled garden of St. Catherine Labouré, just around the corner on rue de Babylone and behind her shrine. Dedicate a full day for this inner-city pilgrimage on the bustling Left Bank, taking the time to absorb the blessings these Parisian sanctuaries offer. When we first started our research on our book, we had little previous knowledge of the Virgin Mary's numerous appearances in France over the centuries. Of course, we knew about Lourdes, where she appeared to Bernadette Soubirous 18 times in 1858, but we were warned that Lourdes was "like Disneyland," crowded with people and quite commercial. Wanting to see it for ourselves, we traveled to this mega-shrine in the foothills of the Pyrenees, where Our Lady of Lourdes receives six million pilgrims each year.

There were large crowds and countless vendors of religious trinkets, but we also experienced a tangible grace when we sought out quiet chapels and crypts. It was an inspiration to see diverse cultures from around the world congregating in one holy place. With the Virgin Mary's presence and untold millions praying here over the past hundred years, how could this sanctified ground not bestow blessings? In spite of the crowds, no spiritual traveler in France should miss the personal experience of Lourdes.

A contrast to Lourdes is the small town of Nevers (pronounced "Neh vay") in Burgundy, one of our favorite regions due to its picturesque countryside and quaint villages. The Convent of St. Gildard, now known as Espace Bernadette Soubirous Nevers, is where St. Bernadette of Lourdes spent the last 13 years of her life and where her body is enshrined. We spent one night at the pilgrim lodging at the convent and wished we could have stayed longer. It was touching to walk the very halls of the convent where St. Bernadette lived, and to spend time in the gardens, and get a small taste of community life. We meditated in the Chapel of St. Bernadette and ate our meals alongside the sisters, sensing always a sacred presence. Nevers is an inspiring stop for one day, and it would be our first choice for a quiet place for an extended retreat.

We found the spiritual life of France hidden, for the most part, yet there is a religious revival among the youth of Europe that is finding expression in rural Burgundy. We had heard of the religious community of Taizé and were curious to see it in action. The goal of the community is to expose retreatants to openness, love, and prayer, and then send them back to their homes around the world to act as creators of peace and reconciliation. Taizé was founded in 1940 when Brother Roger left his native Switzerland to find a place to start a community founded in love. Today, there are as many as 6,000 young people participating each week in the summer programs at Taizé. They learn to experience their own spirituality through daily scriptural study, service, and three periods of meditation and prayer. We visited for the afternoon and were impressed by the young people, their energy for service, and the inwardness of the meditation services. Witnessing thousands of young people eagerly participating in this life-affirming endeavor strengthened our hope for the future.

The region of Normandy in northwestern France is best known for its many tourist sites, but the pilgrim can find solace in the abbey church at Mont Saint-Michel. As we drove west through the rolling green hills, a tall, distant spire suddenly pierced the pastoral view. Moments later, we saw the silhouette of Mont Saint-Michel appear like a castle in the sky, a mystical mirage floating in the clouds. As we arrived at the island abbey, our excitement waned as we discovered a mob of people and tourist shops crowding the narrow streets. A thousand years old, Mont Saint-Michel is now more of a tourist destination than a place of pilgrimage, yet we found the climb to the top well worth our while. The Monastic Fraternity of Jerusalem, men and women who ensure that prayers are being said at all times in the abbey, were preparing for mass as we climbed the hundreds of steps to the abbey church. The sun streaming in through the high gothic windows drew our hearts and eyes upward, and the white-cloaked nuns kneeling on the floor began to chant, filling the church with the most heavenly vibrations. Drawn to tears, we were transported to another time and place. . . .

In France, the power of a holy place is tangible — all you have to do is slow down, relax, and feel. By all means, visit the glistening tourist spots in Paris, the Riviera, and the Alps, but also find time to nurture your soul, and experience the hidden gems of France's many sacred destinations.

52

Finding Myself Amidst the Landscape of Others: The Art of Intentional Travel

by Kendall Dudley, M.A.

Kendall Dudley, M.A., directs Lifeworks Career & Life Design in Belmont, Massachusetts, through which he leads multimedia life-story programs, retreats, and intentional-travel trips abroad. He's taught at Tufts and Lesley Universities, consulted to Harvard for 15 years, and presents on creativity and life direction at national conferences. His public art and social-justice projects received support from the Massachusetts Cultural Council, among others. He is program chair for the Life Planning Network's New England chapter and a contributor to their book, *Live Smart After 50!* Dudley has degrees from the Wharton School and Columbia and was in Peace Corps/Iran. www.kendalldudley.com

We are waiting as others mount their camels before setting out for the Bedouin camp. I hear Anna, one of the women on our trip, cry out in terror as her camel balks. "Hold on tight, you'll be fine!" our guide calls out. Anna wails and hugs the saddle. We are all concerned. "You can walk if you like . . . there's a footpath," I say. "No, no. I have to do this," she says, determined.

After a while, we are quiet as we move through the endless turning of dunes, pushed by the wind, reconfiguring themselves by the moment. Aware of being in a symbolic landscape whose signs I can't comprehend, I feel fully alive.

At night, in our Bedouin tent, we are dining on fragrant goat tagine when Anna tells us that she's come on this trip to ride camels. "When I was a child, I was trampled by wild horses and have been terrified of large animals ever since. I had to get on that camel today." We celebrate the courage it's taken her to do this. Who can know the stories we each carry? The air is now alive with conversation. I say, "Anna makes me want to tackle my own fear of water — I'm imprisoned by it." Another adds, "Anxiety is who I am! But for the first time, I'm not anxious about a thing. I wouldn't have known until now I could be this peaceful." We talk as though being in this tent, at this time, is why we all came to Morocco.

I am leading this band of eight Americans on a trip of self-discovery. We are all professionals over 50, and wondering what we will do once we stop working. Two of us will retire at year's end, one already has, and the rest, like the others, are seeking useful signposts. Meanwhile, equipped with journals, daily writing exercises, and intense curiosity about our own changing winds, we write about what we see and say.

I fall asleep aware of the wind and the stars covering me. I get up around 4:00 a.m. to pee, and watch myself in moonlight standing in the dunes. It's chilly, and gusts of wind blow through me. I take a handful of sand and hold it. I have the idea of taking some home and being buried with it. It is only when I am out of the wind that I realize tears have formed in my eyes. My body knows more about my fears and needs than I let on to myself. Morocco plants me in my body.

Days later, we land at the fabled hill-village of Ait Ben Haddou, a UNESCO site of carved, tapering towers that shoot up from thick walls. Sculpted adobe houses, corrals, and palms hug the hillside. It is late afternoon as we wander up into the maze. Like the desert, this village is composed of iconic forms that seem to be pathways to the unconscious. Tracing the architectural roots to sub-Saharan and Malian architecture only fuels my thinking that West Africa has links to knowledge systems that the West has lost or perhaps has yet to encounter.

We come upon urban men and women in spandex, filming scenes of Jesus and Mary for Moroccan TV. As I watch two actors rehearse, I wonder how I would tell my own story. How would I delineate the chapters, and which episodes would I see as seminal? Looking out at the evening sky, I feel a certain peace, though it's etched with worry that I won't use my remaining years to their fullest. I look for signs all around me, signs that may be metaphors for what I can't see directly.

As we cross the High Atlas, I open my journal to describe the layers of Morocco that are everywhere, reminding me that the future, past, and present are colliding all the time . . . if I can only discern what is vital from what is showy and short-lived!

Finally, we arrive at Marrakech! Dropping our bags at our *riad* (pensione), we walk towards the Djemaa el-Fna, the town square whose Arabic name suggests open space, religion, and death. We pass through sections of the bazaar selling carpets, drums, and stringed instruments, and farther on, cloth, spices, and ice cream. We are then released into the wide sea of space and people that forms the Djemaa el-Fna. It is late afternoon, and families are strolling, drawn to the juice wagons and food stalls. Club Med clients peer at acrobats and snake charmers, while circles of Moroccans hang on the words of storytellers and trance healers. Actors, some in drag, lure us into their audience. This city square is theater on a grand scale, full of history and pageant, ritual and substance. But which is which? No matter what I have read, this place cannot be anticipated in any meaningful way. It is its own fiction and reality, and it is my intention to decipher what all this elicits in me.

It scares me to think how much habit and security have played roles in my evolution. The life of this square suggests alternative realities that my rationalist culture has kept from me. Berbers, Africans and Arabs, Saharan shamans, Europeans, and Moroccans all meet in this cacophony. How am I to divine my way through it? To my Western eyes, the Djemaa is a representation of the id, the unfiltered and untamed, that may yet become a source of insight and passion for me.

An amulet maker prepares a brass capsule for me

into which he pushes bits of bird wing, metals, spices, myrrh, and silver dust. Each component is a link to some belief and heritage of place and culture. Morocco is teaching me to imagine a larger multisource palette from which to choose the components of my life. To discern what they are, I will have to "travel" farther, by reading, journaling, discussing — and by letting go of assumptions as to how my life has to be.

I realize that the act of traveling to other places provides a necessary friction that helps me encounter myself in unanticipated ways. It updates me about my interests, fears, values, and desires. To make this trip in my armchair instead — with my journals, photo albums, camera, drawing materials, and Internet access — I'd need to introduce sources of friction that help me make those unexpected and all-important self-connections. I'd have to ask provocative questions, let curiosity about the future override fear of it, allow myself to potentially reformulate my world view, and rethink the nature of the "work" I have yet to do. And, finally, my search will necessitate revisiting the people, events, and places that I've loved and that have shaped me. Therein will lie the tools to construct my way. Whether in a bus seat, armchair, or both, it's a vivid ride!

53

Enrich Your Travel by Making a Local Connection

by Barbara Weibel

After years of working at unfulfilling jobs, a serious illness made Barbara Weibel realize she felt like the proverbial "hole in the donut" — solid on the outside but empty on the inside. She promised herself that if she recovered, she would reinvent herself as a travel writer and photographer. A year later, fully recovered, she made good on that promise by setting off on a round-the-world trip and starting her blog, www.holeinthedonut.com. These days she travels perpetually, moving from country to country, learning about other cultures and writing about her experiences wherever she can find a Wi-Fi connection.

In Nepal, special ceremonies called *pujas* are held to celebrate the naming of a newborn child, a child's first haircut, a wedding, a person's 84th birthday, and to commemorate the passing of a relative. Since being "adopted" by my Nepali family three years ago, I have had the opportunity to attend many of these ceremonies, but the most fascinating of all was the B*ibaha* P*uja* (marriage ceremony) for my Bahini's (little sister's) nephew.

We left Pokhara as the sun was rising, destined for Bahini's ancestral village of Lekhnath, about an hour down the road. By the time we arrived at the home of the groom's parents, festivities were in full swing. A traditional band of musicians squatted on the ground, horns bellowing and drums booming, as guests made their way to the backyard, where the groom was seated on a chair. He was dressed in the traditional white *daura suruwal*, a specially woven outfit made out of dhaka fabric, with a regular suit jacket on top. On his head he wore a *topi*, the national hat of Nepal, and around his neck hung an elaborately woven necklace of Dubo grass. This grass necklace, known as a D*ubo ko mala*, symbolizes an everlasting relationship because Dubo grass will grow without roots. Family members dipped their fingers into colored powders and rice carefully arranged on a silver tray and pressed a *tika* onto the forehead of the groom before accepting a gift from the groom's father. Meanwhile, women were running around, shoving plates of food in everyone's hands. I wasn't very hungry, but I picked at the *sel roti* fried-rice rings and tooth-breakingly hard, overly sweet rice balls that are traditionally served at a wedding, and was later glad I had. The plan had been for me to stay at the groom's house all day with Bahini, but somehow I got swept up in the crowd and ended up on one of the buses that were bound for Chitwan, the home of the bride and location of the wedding ceremony.

For hours, we sweltered and jounced over rough potholed roads carved into the mountainside alongside a spectacular gorge. I held my breath each time a truck approached from the opposite direction, envisioning our big pink bus plummeting thousands of feet to the river below as we inched ever closer to the edge. Through it all, the band played uninterrupted, perched on the roof of the bus, until we finally arrived at the Hindu temple in Chitwan.

I followed the groom and his entourage up to the second-floor pavilion and muscled my way into the center of the room where the groom was seated. Arms reached out and pulled me aside to make way for the bride. Dressed in an exquisite green-and-red sari, her face covered with a jewel-studded green-and-red-lace veil, she was slowly escorted to the center of the room by her two attendants. In keeping with tradition, her eyes remained downcast and her countenance was sad; I couldn't help but wonder if the requisite sadness had something to do with the fact that this marriage, as with most in Nepal, was arranged. Prior to the wedding, the bride may have only met her intended once, perhaps twice.

The groom stood to meet his bride and she circled him three times, pouring water from a silver pot on the floor before her. The couple faced one another, and a second *Dubo ko mala* was unwrapped and handed to the bride. To loud applause from the onlookers, she tied it around the groom's neck, covering the one he was wearing. The groom then removed his garland and tied it around the bride's neck. This was followed by an exchange of wedding rings, again accompanied by cheers from the guests.

For the next several hours, prayers, anointing, vow taking, and gift giving continued uninterrupted. Since the bride had no father, her uncle (the eldest male head of her household) ceremoniously placed *tikas* on the foreheads of all members of the groom's family and presented gifts to them as an expression of gratitude that the groom had consented to the marriage. The most important male members of the groom's family received gold rings, and all the men received a *topi*. Additionally, every guest of the groom's family received an envelope of cash. Even I, as an adopted member of the extended family, was honored with a *tika* and gift of cash.

Meanwhile, on the lower level of the temple, guests feasted at a sumptuous banquet and danced with abandon as the band played on. As dusk was gathering, the bride's dowry — armoire, bed, end tables, bedding, refrigerator, and television — was loaded atop one of the buses as guests clambered aboard for the trip back to Lekhnath. Hours later, we pulled up to the groom's home, where a wild party was underway. One person at a time stepped into a dimly lit circle and danced to the rhythmic beat of drummers, turning in circles with gracefully extended, floating arms. I hid in the dark fringes, but the family wasn't about to let me off so easily. Hand over hand, I was sent to the front, where the guests insisted I dance. Embarrassed by my sandals and khaki pants in the midst of all the jeweled saris and *kurtas* (collarless shirts), I twirled a few times in my clumsy way and when joyful applause broke out, I fled back into the black anonymity of the night.

Finally, the newlyweds arrived and the groom's mother greeted them with great ceremony, applying a *tika* to their foreheads and making an offering of fruit and incense. The bride took one long step over the threshold, where she would begin her life as a married woman, living in a home she had never seen, with people she did not know. While the couple retired to their wedding chamber, the guests danced wildly and long into the night, celebrating the union.

In Nepal, they have a saying: "Marriage first, love later." Though love marriages are becoming more common, most marriages are still arranged by the families. More than 90 percent of the young women I spoke with in Nepal indicated that they preferred an arranged marriage to a love marriage. It is mind-boggling to my Western way of thinking, but it seems to work for them, and there may be something to the idea that parents know better who is a suitable spouse for their child.

54

How to Walk Your Talk: Traveling with Connection

by Taryn Walker, MS

Taryn Walker, MS, has lived in China, Mexico, and Canada as well as all over the United States, so it is in her blood to travel and explore. She is the Chief Exploration Operator of To Walk Your Talk Travel, which started eight years ago, and she hasn't looked back since. Taryn has degrees in outdoor recreation and in environmental education (with a focus on educational philosophy). Visit: towalkyourtalktravel.com or on Facebook.

Travel has always been a passion of mine. And now I feel privileged to share the joy of discovering the world by taking people on customized trips through my travel business, To Walk Your Talk Travel. My mission is to provide adventurers with an immersive experience so that they can get to know other cultures and to understand our common bonds as well as unique differences. These trips are perfect for retirees who are seeking to know a place from the inside out. By putting ourselves in new environments, we can grow in ways that are often unimaginable.

As we travel and have new experiences together, we figure out how to interact in an authentic way. By going outside of our comfort zones, we create a bridge to understanding. Sometimes this level of communication happens without a shared verbal language, but instead by relying on hand motions, pantomime, smiles, and body language. Often great joy follows as genuine connections are made.

Traveling without the distractions of technology, allowing for a "back to basics" experience, can be magical. For retirees, this kind of getaway can be a great way to transition into the next chapter of their lives. Instead of being caught up in the workplace, what becomes most important are the daily interactions with the others they are traveling with, as well as the people we meet along the way. Every day is a unique adventure. Personally, I feel I reach a level of spiritual connection while in a different country; the stresses of "real life" fade away. With such simplicity, I am rejuvenated.

I have taken groups to India, Nepal, New Zealand, Bali, Kenya, Europe, and Central and South America. In Peru, we spent a week at a Spanish-language school, did open-market shopping, and cooked traditional meals, all while seeing the countryside on the highest train in the Andes. Then we visited medical clinics in the Amazon rainforest and took in the incredible sights of Machu Picchu.

In each case, my mission is to create a genuine connection through shared experiences; both with fellow travelers as well as the communities we visit. Ultimately, everybody on the trip is looking to be enriched by a further understanding of our world and each other. We end most days tired, but excited for the next morning to arrive. I do my best to make sure the travelers have lots of fun by seizing the moment! (Who knows if we will ever be back to this location again, so now is the time.) I thrive on beginning with a specific traveler's bucket list, and then turning it into a meaningful way to learn and grow around the world.

For many retirees, the question, "What do we do now?" looms large. So besides visiting a new place we also like to contribute something worthwhile to the town or village while we are there. Volunteerism is integrated into our journeys whenever possible. The types of projects vary from country to country. I like creating opportunities to incorporate a sense of traveling with intention wherever we go, so it is about much more than just seeing sights. I believe that "giving back" should be designed by the communities. We often spend time in "family homestay," where we learn to cook local foods and view family interactions in a way that tourists don't get to see.

Susan, a retired accountant, had several big items on her bucket list and was thinking about the need to find a new sense of purpose. On a trip with me to Costa Rica, she discovered what a treat it was to experience a homestay. She said she loved zip-lining in the rainforest and white-water rafting, but what thrilled her the most was when she helped our group to build a fifty-foot concrete sidewalk in a small village. That was the most gratifying activity of all.

One of the growing trends in travel is ancestry tourism for retirees. Many people in their later years seek to connect with their heritage and traditions, not just by doing research online but by taking a trip to the country where their ancestors had once lived. In 2011, I visited

Neuchâtel, Switzerland with my brother and sister on such a journey. My brother had found a document written by my great-grandfather in which he referred to our family tree. We found out that our family was Swiss instead of German, which is what we had always been told. For us to be able to visit a town with a castle on the side of a mountain overlooking a grand lake, and to look at its beauty and the people from the perspective of tracing our roots, was a wonderful experience. While there, we saw a painting of a villager that had very similar features to our family line. We could have been looking at an uncle or grandfather!

If you are thinking about walking in the footsteps of your ancestors, learning more about where you come from and forming a deeper connection beyond the Web sites you have researched, let's start planning! You will be able to see where your relatives lived and perhaps meet others to whom you may be related. Some retirees turn this into an adventure for their whole family, bringing along their adult children and grandchildren or siblings. Perhaps ancestry travel will be the newest item for your bucket list!

55

Tales of the Tombs in Israel

by Judith Fein

Judith Fein is an award-winning travel journalist, playwright, screenwriter, theater director, speaker, author, and filmmaker. She has contributed travel articles to more than 100 publications and Web sites, blogs for the Huffington Post and *Psychology Today*, and is the cofounder/editor of www.YourLifeIsaTrip.com. With her photojournalist husband, Paul Ross, she specializes in cultural travel, and teaches travel writing and photography. Fein has lived in Europe and North Africa and lives to leave. Her Web site is www.GlobalAdventure.us.

I was in Israel on a personal mission. I was born and raised Jewish, but I was disaffected from institutional Judaism. Over the past few decades, I had bathed my soul in the spiritual waters of many different traditions, but, for me, the world of synagogues and formal, standardized prayer books was dry and uninspiring. I longed for deep connection; I wanted to be stirred, moved, and transported to transcendent realms. It hadn't happened for me in America, but maybe it would happen

This essay is an excerpt from Judith Fein's book *Life Is a Trip: The Transformative Magic of Travel* and is reprinted with permission.

in Israel. So, even though the media assaulted us with daily images of Arabs and Jews attacking, shooting, bombing, and threatening to kill each other, I was determined to find out if there was anything spiritual, mystical, healing, and holy in the Holy Land.

That is what had brought me and my husband, Paul, to the town of Safed in the area known as the Galilee, in the north of Israel. Although he had little interest in religion, holiness, or other affairs of the spirit (he dismissively lumped all of it under the heading of superstition), Paul had agreed to photograph whatever I found.

"This is where legendary rabbis inspired the Hebrew people thousands of years ago. It is also where, in the medieval period, brilliant rabbis developed and disseminated the mystical Torah studies known as Kabbalah," our guide, Nurit, told us.

The hills around Safed are dotted with ancient tombs. To Jewish believers, these tombs of long-deceased *tzaddikim*, or holy men, are the meeting place between the living and the dead. People make pilgrimages to the burial places to ask for blessings, favors, surcease from suffering.

"They do not actually pray to the ancient rabbis; rather, they pray that the departed *tzaddikim* will intercede on their behalf with God," Nurit explained. "And because God looks favorably upon holy men and the merit of their lives, he is more likely to grant a request."

I wanted the hills surrounding Safed to be a spiritual place for me, but at the tomb of Rabbi Uziel, I was interested and amused, not inspired. Paul came out of the men's side (men and women are separated in Orthodox Judaism), and when I asked him what had happened, he tersely responded, "Nothing."

Nevertheless, I decided to visit one other grave in the small, ancient village of Meron — perched on the side of Mount Meron, with its abundant greenery, trees, and views of Safed and the Galilee. Meron village is the resting place of Shimon bar Yochai. One of the most famous of the *tzaddikim*, he is credited with being the author of the central book of Kabbalah, called the Zohar, almost 2,000 years ago. Believers go to his grave to pray for prosperity, peace in their souls, fertility, and healing.

Paul and I climbed up the narrow main street of Meron to two stone archways with Hebrew inscriptions (one arch for men and one for women) that led to the whitewashed *tsyun*, a building made of local rocks, cement, earth, and stones that houses the remains of the famed first-century (C.E.) rabbi, Jonathan ben Uziel.

Paul entered the men's section, looked around, shot a few photos, shrugged, and exited. "Don't ask. Nothing happened," he said pointedly. "Nothing."

But for me, things would be very different and unexpected.

As soon as I entered the women's side of the *tsyun*, my body started to shake and I began to sob. I looked around, self-conscious. A few women sat on benches and others stood facing the walls or the tomb itself, praying. No one was paying any attention to me as I wept, drenching the front of my pale blue shirt. I walked — no, I wove to the tomb, placed my head on the cool, white exterior, and prayed and cried for healing for my thinning bones. And I felt as though — how can I describe this? — I felt as though my words were heard.

***

When I came home, I started to notice people all around me who yearned to be moved in their souls. Some of them were transported by music. Others by nature or art, cooking or ministering to their elders.

I felt a longing to be connected to the dead, to transcend the boundaries of time and space. I bought a *yahrzeit* candle, which is the commemorative candle-in-a-glass that Jewish people light every year on the anniversary of the death of their near and dear ones.

After dinner, when the phones weren't ringing and my computer was in sleep mode, I lit the candle and began to talk to my father, Eddie, who died when I was young. His passing left a deep, unfillable hole. Not only had he been deprived of a full life, but I had spent all of my adult existence without a father.

First, I told him what was going on in my life. I spoke about my work, my marriage to Paul, how my mother was doing. I said I had been to Israel where I visited the tombs of the rabbis. I talked freely about this and that, and then I began to ask him questions. "Are you okay?" "Are you at peace?" "Are you watching over us?" "Do you think I am doing the right thing with my life?"

All of the questions could be answered by "yes" or "no." And I swear to you that when the answer was "yes," the flame of the candle grew bigger. And when the reply was "no," the flame flitted horizontally from side to side.

Was I imagining it? I don't think so. Is it really that easy for the living to access the deceased? If both parties are willing, I believe the answer is "yes."

Maybe I just have faith or a yearning in my soul to connect to something larger than me. If you have faith, you may want to try it.

56

The Adventure Spa with Spirit

by Kristina Hurrell

Kristina Hurrell founded SpaFari in 2003. Her global "fitness adventures" have inspired and empowered individuals, groups, corporations, and celebrities in all areas of health, fitness, wellness, spirituality, and passionate living. She began her career as a top fashion model and actress in Europe and the United States, and progressed with architecture, interior design, an active-sportswear company, a destination spa, health and self-management curricula for colleges, plus private (phone) life-coaching sessions. She and her award-winning company have been featured in many editorials and appear regularly on national TV and radio shows.

Whoop, RETIREMENT! As Jack Nicholson has been heard to say, "Ya just gotta love it, pal!"

There's a lot to get excited about. You have time to take on creative ideas and passions. Time to think a little deeper, and tweak your consciousness a little higher.

Time to grow wisdom and life experience, and time to plunge into adventurous living.

Preparing to step out with gusto means a shake-up of focus, a time to ante up on health and wellness. The benefits you'll receive from following the discipline of daily healthy guidelines will give you an added boost. You'll show up in life more fully, enjoy it longer, and embrace a richness of quality that previous generations never dreamed possible.

> *"Life is like riding a bicycle. To keep your balance you must keep moving."* — Albert Einstein

Stepping into this new chapter of your life might mean you feel called to journey into the world as an active and vibrant traveler. Many retirees are looking to combine travel with fitness opportunities that get results. They want to have fun and variety without the risk of injury, to stay in shape, and to feel confident that their exercise workout won't threaten their balance or other existing health conditions. Many realize the importance of overcoming the fear of injury, which could develop into an excuse to avoid exercise altogether.

It was in meeting the demands of age-appropriate, safe, and effective travel that I created Ageless Active Vacations, a specific program within my company, SpaFari, that offers trips for boomers and seniors with a heightened emphasis on rejuvenation. These trips are geared to promote a foundation of health and well-being, longevity, and independence.

For each SpaFari adventure, we do intense research to make sure the hiking trails, location, and weather are going to be suitable before offering the program to clients. And so it was, while on an initial site-inspection trip to Lake Como, Italy, that I made a rather amazing discovery. A particularly inviting wilderness trail started off part cobblestone, part mossy earth, and ended in the mountains at a waterfall flowing adjacent to a dilapidated monastery. Stone chunks, probably the remains of a building wall, covered the ground. I felt as if I were entering a world of long ago.

Surveying the scene while munching my packed lunch, I suddenly bristled. A presence. Swiveling, I caught sight of two blinking eyes through a thicket of bushes. Then, crashing out of them and braying, an old donkey trapped me against the rubble, menacingly exposing yellowed teeth. My yelling "Shoo, shoo" only heightened the crazed beast's aggression . . . until it swung back to bite the heavy boot of a scraggly, bearded old man who kicked its backside. Between profanities, the stranger smiled apologies. Gratefully sharing my lunch with him, I inquired about his presence there, all alone, and in halting English, French, and Italian he told me this story:

Many hundred years ago, a blind, deaf, dumb, and crippled child playing in the earth touched a stone that turned out to be an ancient relic of a statue of baby Jesus. Pulling it free from the ground, the child instantly received a healing. The monastery was built at the site, and the relic was placed in its chapel. As its fame spread, throngs of people made pilgrimages up the mountain, and many were healed while praying in its presence. Even troubled lake sailors claimed to have been saved after having a vision of the relic and praying.

When a king of Venice requested the relic, the monks refused to give it to him. Consequently, soldiers arrived with orders for the monks to renounce their faith, or be executed. All were executed. The relic disappeared. Over time, the monastery fell to ruin.

Fast forward to 60-odd years ago. A ten-year-old boy from Milan began dreaming he was one of the executed monks. Now, in later years, his life has become a pilgrimage to rebuild the monastery. His sole companion is the difficult donkey.

As the old man finished his story and we were about to part, he directed me to take a different route downward to a church that now houses the statue of the baby Jesus. It sat protected in a gated room, surrounded by silver hearts of gratitude from those who had been healed while praying in its presence.

Each Lake Como trip I make with my SpaFari group always includes a hike up to visit my monk friend — still busy repairing the monastery — and later down to the church and statue.

Many historical tales gleaned from the area are shared with clients who stay at our lovely family-run Hotel Belvedere in Bellagio, considered to be the "pearl" of Lake Como. Each room opens out to sparkling lake views and the beauty of the surrounding countryside: chateaux, olive groves, picturesque fishing villages, and the snowcapped Alps and Dolomites in the distance.

Most early mornings, I lead the yoga-stretch class in an elegant marbled room, and after a healthy breakfast, I accompany the group for a day of adventure and discovery. Ferry rides take us to destinations around the lake from which we hike, the trails alive with wildflowers and little goat bells. The SpaFari guides who lead us include Italian naturalists knowledgeable about the region.

I personally organize the villa chefs to prepare our healthy, packed lunches, which we enjoy trailside with 360-degree vistas; other days, we eat at little hamlet bistros. Afternoons include cultural explorations of neoclassical villas and their gardens, and an afternoon shopping expedition to the lively town of Como, famous for its silk factories.

Three afternoon massages are included in the eight-day trip, with optional beauty treatments at the villa spa. Clients are encouraged to swim at the villa pool to help loosen their muscles after hiking.

Over the years, I've made acquaintances with chefs at the picturesque lakeside restaurants, arranging our healthy dinners, with dietary restrictions factored into selections.

Some evenings we enjoy chamber music at the grand Villa Serbelloni; on others, I offer talks on wellness, nutrition, healthy aging, stress management, perfect digestion, and "sage-ing." This chapter in our lives is a golden opportunity to share wisdom, love, experience, and deep thoughts with younger generations. We can join them to help change the quality of our environment: by growing seasonable vegetables, becoming an advocate against foods derived from GMOs (genetically modified organisms), and driving eco-friendly cars. For true happiness comes from the joy of deeds well done, and the zest of exchanging ideas and creating new experiences.

I've found that all our SpaFari trips inspire our clients to live more fulfilling lives, and with Ageless Active Vacations we encourage our travelers to change the image of retirement. To do this, let us uplift our spirit and awaken our passion. Live fully present in each moment and embrace our precious age. Because right now is the oldest and the youngest we'll ever be again.

57

A Journey to Self-Understanding

by John E. Nelson

John E. Nelson is coauthor of *What Color Is Your Parachute? For Retirement*. His work has been covered in the *New York Times*, *The Wall Street Journal*, *USA Today*, and elsewhere. Nelson has led workshops for the federal government, the United Way, AARP, college alumni associations, and *Fortune* "100 Best Companies" employers.

Why are you reading a book about travel?

Whether you can actually take any of the trips described in this book isn't all that important, to be honest. If you're able to travel, that will be wonderful. But if you aren't, and need to content yourself with only reading about travel, that's okay, too.

In fact, the most interesting journey in this book just might be the journey to understanding yourself. Understanding why travel is important to you, and what you value most in life, is a trip in itself. Where, how, and with whom you would like to travel are all clues to your deepest motivations. Seeing what is important to you about travel helps you see what is most significant to you in your life. And isn't retirement supposed to be about discovering and doing what's meaningful to you?

A famous researcher at Hebrew University, Shalom Schwartz, has spent the last 25 years measuring what values people all around the world find most meaningful and motivating in their lives. His research surveys have been translated into over 30 languages, and he's gathered data in over 60 countries. His theory — Values Theory — is the epitome of a world traveler!

What has he discovered? It turns out that all around the world, people recognize the same ten basic value orientations in themselves and others. But, while people would agree on what those ten values are, they disagree about which ones are most important. So, choosing from these ten values will help you decide what's most essential to you in planning for your trips. And it will also provide you with insights for planning your whole retirement stage of life.

First, think about the kind of travel that most excites you.

Where do you want to go? How would you get there? What would you do before, during, and after? Who would you take with you? What kind of trips would really motivate you to invest the time, money, and energy needed?

Now, keep some of these travel ideas in mind while you look through the ten basic values below. The list is organized so the values that are most similar to each other are listed closest together. Then, when you get to the end, number ten is most similar to number one. They connect back into one big circle. Here they are:

1. Self-Direction: *Independent thought and action, and having the freedom to choose, create, and explore.* For example, do you yearn to break free, and travel to do your own thing, with no one judging you for it?

2. Stimulation: *Excitement, novelty, challenge, and seeking variety and change.* For example, do you get excited about going to a place you've never been before, or doing an activity you've never done before?

3. Hedonism: *The pleasure of enjoying sensual pursuits, and self-indulgence.* For example, do you relish the idea of a trip just for pure enjoyment, just for yourself?

4. Achievement: *Demonstrating success and competence, and* *reaching your goals.* For example, do you plan to attain something through your travels, or accomplish some endeavor?

5. Power: *Social status and prestige, material possessions and money.* For example, do you demand the best accommodations and services, and do you travel by first class?

6. Security: *Personal and family safety, along with social stability and national security.* For example, is safety and cleanliness important to you when you travel, regardless of where you go and what you do?

7. Conformity: *Meeting social responsibilities, showing respect and politeness to people you know.* For example, whatever trip you undertake, is it important for you to exercise restraint and preserve harmony among your traveling companions?

8. Tradition: *Commitment to culture or religion, and preserving time-honored customs.* For example, are you drawn to visit places or events that connect you with your upbringing or beliefs?

9. Benevolence: *Helping, supporting, and loving the people who are close to you.* For example, do you think less about travel for your own sake, and more about how your travel can enhance the lives of your friends or family?

10: Universalism: *Understanding and appreciating the welfare of all people and of nature.* For example, do you seek to encounter new people and places in a nonjudgmental way, and to express concern for their welfare?

As you read through each of the ten values, your initial reaction may be that you're motivated by many of them. There are some times when you may feel every one of these applies to you! But then as you revisit each of the ten, you'll discover that only a few represent ongoing themes in your life. You might recognize that some of these values used to be important to you in the past, but you've let go of them and they don't motivate you now. Or that you've been clinging to some out of habit, but they're not really important anymore. You've changed, and you're ready to move on. In the end, when you make your choices, you'll know that only two or three of them are truly meaningful for you.

Once you've taken your journey to self-understanding, and you know your motivating values — what do you do with them? At the very least, you can arrange and prioritize your travel according to what will be most fulfilling and meaningful for you. And at the very most, you can arrange and prioritize your retirement stage of life that way, too.

Bon voyage!

58

Thin Places

by Sharon Gilchrest O'Neill, Ed.S., LMFT

Sharon Gilchrest O'Neill, Ed.S., LMFT, is a licensed marriage and family therapist and the author of A *Short Guide to a Happy Marriage* and its *Gay Edition*, as well as *Sheltering Thoughts About Loss and Grief*, and *Lur'ning: 147 Inspiring Thoughts for Learning on the Job*. She has worked for over 30 years, both in private practice and the corporate setting, helping her clients to examine assumptions, think creatively, and build upon strengths. O'Neill holds three degrees in psychology, is a clinical fellow of AAMFT, and maintains a private practice in Westchester County, New York. She is often called on as an expert by a variety of print/online publications, including the *New York Times*, the *Boston Globe*, and *The Wall Street Journal*. www.ashortguidetoahappymarriage.com

I have forever been drawn to the ocean. Not for swimming or sailing or surfing, but for simply sinking heavy into an ocean's vast presence, and allowing its peaceful power to wash over me. I am able to lose myself in a way that cannot happen elsewhere. Time stands still.

For years, I traveled to Cape Cod to get my ocean "fix." Then, through a chance investigation of East Coast dunes, I found myself planning a surprise wedding-anniversary trip for my husband to North Carolina. We were headed just south of the Virginia border to one of the more remote 13 miles of dunes of the Outer Banks. On this first visit to the 4x4 beaches, we arrived in the daylight, as is recommended for newcomers. Traveling on the beach and over the dunes (there are no paved roads) to your rental home in the dark (there are no streetlights) can be daunting, if not precarious, for those without experience.

The moment we left the paved road, having lowered the air pressure in the tires of our 4-wheel drive, we were in awe. We knew we had found a very special place. As we maneuvered the nine miles of beach to our rental home, the palette before us was quite remarkable: a fantastically wide-open ocean of bright blues and violets gently buffeting golden sands of myriad patterns. There were cotton-candy clouds floating high above and mysterious-looking tree stumps rising boldly out of the swale. We would later learn these stumps are remnants of maritime forests, and depending on the tides, they might capture treasures for a beachcomber like me.

And then there were the magnificent horses to behold: wild, yet docile. We encountered several groups cooling themselves at the water's edge or grazing on beach grasses, their manes blowing enchantingly in the ocean breezes. Quite simply, we were wonderstruck. Over the years, we have watched these descendants of Spanish Mustangs mate and birth their foals just as they have done for 500 years on these dunes.

Bouncing along in our SUV that first time, we had a genuine feeling of leaving everything behind and journeying onward without a care in the world.

Recently, I have learned about the term "Thin Places," and I am certain that I now have my Thin Place in this glorious 13-mile strip of North Carolina Barrier Island. Celtic tradition suggests there are places where the physical world and the spiritual world come so close that the distance between them is thin. Such places are believed to be capable of engendering a more direct experience of spirituality or otherworldliness. Thin Places have been called mystical and magical. They promise enchantment and wonder; they reward with rest and contemplation.

I now appreciate, from the way others have spoken of

transformational places in their lives, that they, too, have their Thin Places: a compound in India, a country home in Ireland, or an inlet cove in Maine. Many believe, most importantly, that these places replenish the spirit and the soul. They calm the chatter in our brain. Thin Places sharpen and stimulate the use of our senses in bright ways. They reward us with fresh perspectives and expanded states of mind. They can spark creativity. They can provoke new dreams or stir old ones.

Thin Places inspire awe. They can take our breath away. Life slows down. There is no hurry. How interesting that research at Stanford University recently found that awe (not joy or any other positive emotion) actually gives us the feeling that time has slowed down and that *we* have slowed down. A full schedule looses its meaning. A watch is a nuisance. And dare I say our personal technology becomes irrelevant?

What a perfect time at 65 and beyond to become better attuned to your needs as you seek out traveling experiences of all sorts, near and far. It seems to me that it is movement through new spaces that affords the chance of stepping right into a Thin Space. So, go somewhere on a whim or on another's suggestion;

take an unusual route in a favorite city; travel with someone different, or travel alone; stroll into that pub a few towns over that you always speculated about; do some day hikes on the Appalachian Trail; test a stay in a lakeside cabin; or travel to the state or country next door.

No one ever knows when they might come upon *their* Thin Place; one can only happen upon it. It is never a plotted journey. Your GPS does not list Thin Places under points of interest. So, cast your fate to your travels and let your Thin Place find you.

And, when you do happen upon it, what you will feel is a relaxation into your most genuine, true self. Such a state of being is one that you can never quite get enough of, and you will yearn to return to this space where all feels right with the world. Keep in mind the very personal nature of such an experience. One individual's Thin Place is another's nightmare. There are all kinds of wondrous Thin Places in the world, some intriguingly simple, others more elaborate. Some may be just around the corner, others halfway 'round the world.

It may also be that you already have a Thin Place hiding in the wings. Somewhere you have longed to go back to for many years, but the time just never seemed right to do so. A place that you have never forgotten that is imbued with the stuff of Thin Places. Make that plan to go back. When will there ever be a better time than now?

Each time I return, I am eternally grateful that I happened upon my place of brilliant sunsets composed of stirring shades of pink and orange, and a beach that stretches on forever. The moment the tires hit the dunes, I know the landscape changes and my life will, too. A stack of books, some good wine, and my walking legs are all that I need. My Thin Place never lets me down; I can always count on taking away with me the gift of a new idea or a most perfect sand dollar to tide me over 'til the next time. In the end, I suspect a part of me will rest here forever.

I wish for you a place of wonder in which to surrender yourself to time slowing down, maybe even standing still for some moments. I am sure many of you have that place and cherish it as I do mine. For those of you who have not yet happened upon your Thin Place, continue looking — you will find your own special place of awe.

Section

HIT THE ROAD, JACK

59

Twenty-five Feet and the Open Road

by Bob Lowry

Bob Lowry was a management consultant to several hundred radio stations before retiring in 2001. He has written two books, authors a successful retirement blog, and lives with his wife in Scottsdale, Arizona. www.satisfyingretirement.blogspot.com.

An estimated eight million RVs are owned or rented by Americans. They come in all shapes and sizes: some only big enough for a double mattress, while others are as large as a bus, with an inside that would put a high-end resort to shame. It's difficult to be on any major highway and not see dozens of these recreational vehicles driving to a new adventure. Not surprisingly, retirees are often behind the wheel.

After years of putting it off, my wife and I finally succumbed to the lure of RV travel last fall. Not wanting to commit to a major purchase before being sure this was right for us, we rented a 25-foot motor home and spent nine days in the White Mountains of northern Arizona.

It was one of the best vacations we have ever taken. We both fell in love with the experience. After 11 years of a very satisfying retirement with plenty of travel, we have discovered the excitement and sense of freedom that an RV offers. We are hooked.

I did worry about being able to drive and maneuver a vehicle three times longer and taller than my car. Nightmares of smashing into a gas station overhang were common in the days before we picked up the RV. Could I hook up the sewer hose properly without covering myself in "black water," the charming RV name for waste water? Would I somehow blow up the electric generator if I used the wrong plug? Could my wife and I be happy in such a small space?

I quickly discovered that setting up an RV is easier than putting up a tent. In less than ten minutes, the sewer line for the toilet, kitchen sink, and shower was in place, fresh water was flowing into the faucets, the refrigerator began cooling the food we had just bought, and the gas stove was ready to cook dinner. The rental dealer gave us a quick demonstration, but I also prepared ahead of time by reading a book and watching a video on what to do.

Avoiding major highways and interstates means a chance to rediscover small-town America. You stumble across picture-perfect main streets, festivals, art shows, and farmers' markets. We found a book sale to support a local library; a dozen new paperbacks fit nicely in the RV. Dinner becomes a salad and bread bought from a roadside stand just hours earlier.

One weekday, a state park was nearby so we pulled in. It was so beautiful and calm that a picnic was almost a requirement. We picked some food from our traveling kitchen, found a tablecloth and two folding chairs, and lunch was ready. Entertainment was provided by a few fishermen on the lake, clouds hanging still in a deep-blue sky, birds diving for fish, and the latest mystery novel by our favorite author. The afternoon seemed to last forever.

Because we had brought a car with us, we were free to leave the RV at the campground and explore the area. One morning, as we finished our breakfast at the picnic table just outside the motor home's door, we decided to drive a few hours to the Grand Canyon. At the Canyon's gift store, we bought a National Parks Passport with listings and maps of every national park and site in the country. Instantly, we had a focus: build our upcoming RV trips around seeing as many of the parks as we could.

Another day, we decided to take a hike though a meadow absolutely teeming with yellow and purple wildflowers. We exchanged greetings with other hikers, bikers, and those walking their dogs. Saturday night in downtown Flagstaff found us and a hundred others at a free movie playing in the town square.

Folks who travel by RV are friendly and helpful. Those who spend a good part of their lives on the road love to talk about their adventures and show off their rolling homes. Putting a bowl of chips and some salsa on the picnic table is an open invitation for others to stop by and chat.

One couple paid us a visit our first night to welcome us to the RV lifestyle. They said they spend every summer in Flagstaff, and then the rest of year they visit their kids and grandkids scattered all over the country. Their permanent home is in Phoenix, but they are only there for a month each year. I wondered if they ever got tired of all that travel. "Absolutely not," the husband told us. "It keeps us young, and we never get bored. I don't have to worry about yard work either."

Many RVers travel with a dog or two: this serves as an easy icebreaker and a source of shared stories. The campgrounds we visited welcomed dogs with special areas for off-leash romps. One even had a dog-grooming area to keep pets clean.

Laundry facilities, convenience stores and gift shops, community campfires, and even swimming pools are common in many modern RV parks. Most offer free Wi-Fi as part of the nightly rate. That was an important bonus. I could spend some time writing for my blog, while my wife edited the hundreds of photos she took each day. Most evenings would find us sitting outside, under the stars, watching a movie streaming to the laptop perched on the picnic table. It was our private drive-in movie.

If you've thought about recreational-vehicle travel but have hesitated, I urge you to give it a try. Today's units are no more difficult to drive than a car, and they're extremely simple to set up. There is something very freeing about this type of travel. The road stretches before you, with the only limits imposed by time and budget. Whenever you stop at the end of the day, everything you need is with you. Living in a small space means you learn to simplify and take just what you need. Cleanup becomes a five-minute chore.

My wife and I find that being so close to nature is invigorating. RV travel allows you to step away from a busy life and have time and space to really relax. Obligations and schedules are left behind.

There is an RV in our future and roads waiting to be explored. It is an experience like no other and now a very important part of my satisfying retirement.

60

Little Bus, Big Bus

by Michael Milone, Ph.D.

Michael Milone, Ph.D., is a research psychologist based in New Mexico. At 67, he runs marathons whenever his knees let him and cross-trains with biking, swimming, skiing, and snowshoeing. On a more creative note, he managed to convince Arena Press to publish three of his novels, all of which are available online.

A lthough I've been a traveling guy for my entire adult life, I stepped it up a little when I reached my 60s and eased back the throttle on my work as a research psychologist just a bit. In addition to traveling more to pursue my interests in running, biking, triathlon, and skiing, I decided to bring others into my devious plan to have as much fun as I could. It was on my first trip to Positano with my wife, some family members, and a few friends that my infatuation with the little bus and big bus began. All of those who traveled with me think I'm the smartest guy on the planet for dragging them along.

As incredible as it seems, two of the most wonderful travel experiences on Earth cost just a few dollars . . . excluding the cost of getting there. One is a bus ride around Positano, Italy, a place whose beauty is simply indescribable. The other is the bus ride to Positano from Sorrento. (Note to readers: Whenever you take a bus or train in Italy, be sure to validate your ticket by inserting it in the little machine just before you get on. The machine will be near the boarding point or on the bus.)

The local bus service in Positano is provided by tiny orange buses that are part of the Flavio Gioia transportation company. As an aside, Flavio Gioia is a legendary figure said to have invented a kind of compass. There is no evidence to support this, but it's a nice story.

Positano is a relatively small town perched on a mountainside above the Mediterranean Sea. Its tiny, winding streets and walkways lead a visitor from one unexpected sight to another, and the people of the town are exceptionally welcoming. The views of the Mediterranean are breathtaking, and the subtle beauty of a tiny stairway from one level of the town to another is just as fulfilling. Finding your way by foot through Positano is sigh inspiring.

On our first visit to Positano, my traveling companions were surprised when I suggested taking the little bus, as all of us enjoyed wandering by foot through the town. They quickly changed their minds, as the bus navigated narrow streets we had not yet discovered and made its way up to Montepertuso and Nocelle, two villages in the mountains above Positano.

When we stopped beside the elementary school, a dozen or so children boarded the already crowded bus. Still dressed in their school clothes, they carried gear and soccer balls. We couldn't imagine where they were going, as the terrain made a soccer field simply impossible.

As the bus climbed the switchbacks, the view alternated between the Mediterranean and the spectacular hillsides, still covered with flowers even though it was late October. The enthusiasm of the schoolchildren increased, and as we turned a corner, an unlikely sight greeted us: a soccer field had been hacked from the side of the mountain. The children left the bus, along with most of the locals, and they joined a throng waiting to start the afternoon's matches.

We continued up the mountain, passing Montepertuso on the way. This geologic feature, a protruding ridge with a hole worn through it, is the evidence of a confrontation between Satan and the Virgin Mary, in which the Fallen Angel came in a dismal second. It was not long before we reached the end of the line, the town of Nocelle.

At this point, you have several choices. One is to take the bus down again, which is a perfectly acceptable option. You'll be surprised at how different the scenery looks on the way down, even though you are traveling mostly on the same roads.

A second option is to get off the bus and walk down. There is a well-marked trail consisting mostly of stone steps that will take you to the center of Positano. This doesn't sound very exciting, but it is a truly unique experience that blends natural and man-made beauty.

Speaking of hikes, Nocelle is at one end of the Sentiero degli Dei, the Path of the Gods. A third option is to spend a little time wandering along this awesome trail. Don't attempt to hike the whole thing. Save that for another day, but it is without doubt one of the world's best walks.

The only real competition for the little orange bus is the big bus from Sorrento to Positano and then on to Amalfi. All of the towns along the bus route are unforgettably charming. I realize that my description sounds like hyperbole, but no one who has been there will disagree.

Now, back to the bus ride. The big blue bus is part of the SITA group that provides transportation throughout Italy. It makes regular round trips between Sorrento and Amalfi, two wondrous places, stopping at many of the small towns in between. For most of the ride, you are on the highway sometimes called the Blue Ribbon, which is *Nastro Azzurro* in Italian. (This is also the name of an Italian beer.)

Within a few minutes, you will be convinced that it is impossible for the driver to keep the bus on the road. At times, you will be peering down more than a thousand feet to the rocky shore of the Mediterranean. If you look out the other side of the bus, you will see a sheer cliff that rises for more than a thousand feet above you. Your sense of panic, which is well deserved, will be ameliorated by an absolutely, positively glorious view of the sea and shoreline.

Your reverie will be short-lived, however, because oncoming traffic, which often includes a truck or another bus, will reestablish the challenge faced by the *autista*, the bus driver. Seeming to defy the laws of physics, your driver and those of the other vehicles will manage to pass one another without incident . . . most of the time.

It is impossible to attempt to describe the sights that you will enjoy on the bus ride between Sorrento and Amalfi. One of my favorites is Le Sirenuse, a cluster of three islands that was the home of the mythical sirens, the most famous of which were Parthenope, Leucosia, and Ligeia. I found the islands so enchanting that I included them in my latest novel, *Juno's Twins*. (Yes, I know it's a shameless plug, but part of the book is set in this region of Italy 3,000 years ago when Rome was founded.)

To get to Positano or Sorrento, the easy way is to fly to Rome or Naples, and either rent a car or hire a car and driver. If you have an adventurous spirit, consider this next possibility, although it sounds totally crazy: Take the train from the Rome airport to the train station in Rome. (It's perfectly acceptable to spend the night in Rome before heading south.) Then, take the train to Naples, and once you arrive, board the little train (Circumvesuviana) to Sorrento. From there, take the blue SITA bus to Positano. When you return home, you will undoubtedly have fantastic tales to tell of the experience of a lifetime.

61

There Is No Such Thing as Taking a Wrong Turn

by Zenaida des Aubris

Born in Argentina, educated in the United States, and living in Europe for more than 30 years, it is no wonder that multilingual Zenaida des Aubris chose a career in opera and classical music management and production. These assignments enabled her to travel the world, including the Far East, South America, and all the European cultural capitals. She now writes for various English and German publications, as well as continuing to travel on her own for the pure enjoyment of discovering her very own uncharted territory.

Have you ever just turned a corner and found yourself in a different world?

Often, going off the beaten track is as easy as that — just turning a corner away from the main road, down an alley, or across a bridge — in order to get off the path pounded by thousands to get to a tourist attraction.

After all, only by finding your way off the beaten track will you be able to incidentally/accidentally discover all sorts of highlights, highways and byways, dead ends and side streets full of charm, treasures, and thrills. Years ago, when Prague was just opening up to the Western world, I was on my way to cross the famous Charles Bridge. It was a sunny September day, and a large pot of red geraniums beckoned to me at the end of an alley, distinctly not on the way to the bridge. Following my instinct, I walked toward the geranium pot and ended up in a dusty antiques shop, every bargain hunter's dream, filled top to bottom with potential treasures. To this day, I cherish a small Art Nouveau table lamp I found there, not only because of the item itself, but because it also brings back memories of the entire little adventure, the thrill of turning away from a predictable path, not knowing what to expect next, talking to the shopkeeper in no language known to man, but both of us understanding each other and taking great enjoyment in the transaction.

Traveling off the beaten track presupposes an open state of mind, where you welcome new impressions and adventures because you are not glued to a route carefully traced in red on your map. Most guided tours will take you from sight to worthwhile sight, all deemed to be "must-see" places. In the end, you can tick off all the Big Bens and Eiffel Towers of the world, but have you really gotten to know the city or country you set out to visit? Isn't it more worthwhile to throw guides and maps overboard and simply wander the streets? Find your own route to the Eiffel Tower through the small streets that lead up to the Champ de Mars, catching glimpses of the iron-latticed wonder through the narrow gaps between buildings. It's better than arriving by conventional tour bus at the parking lot and being herded along by a stressed-out guide. How much more fun and adventuresome to meander through your own uncharted territory, and to reach such destinations not by a straight A to B route but via D, Q, and P! As a bonus, you get many more original photo angles and opportunities.

So, how do you get off the beaten track? A good beginning is to not take a map along, or (if you worry about getting too lost) just bring only the most rudimentary of instructions. Beware of smartphones with their built-in GPS or Google Maps! It might take some discipline on your part to keep from looking up where you are, but believe me, it will pay off in a heightened sense of adventure and fun. And, let's face it, it is comforting to know that help is at hand — or in your pocket — if you really do need it.

Maps and guides also discourage you from interacting with the locals, but asking them questions can add yet another wonderful dimension to getting to know a country and its people. Who has not had the experience of disorientation when coming out of the subway and wondering, which way do I go now? I make it a point to ask a newspaper seller or florist for directions, which I then may or may not follow, based on how much time I have available. I always like taking another walk around a block to give me more of a sense of the neighborhood, its flair, and its people.

Going "across the bridge, then second right, and left again" once got me to a lovely, quiet cul-de-sac in Venice, inhabited only by a couple of cats napping in the sunshine and what seemed like a jungle of crisscrossed lines of washing hung out to dry between the buildings — a photographer's dream setting. Twenty minutes later I was still shooting away, utterly entranced by the play of the wind in the underwear and sheets.

Consider "going off the beaten track" your very own reality show. The real world and your cognitive impressions are bound to be more three-dimensional than any virtual environment, such as a video or podcast, can ever be.

In today's world, doing your own exploring doesn't necessarily mean becoming disoriented — instead, it can lead to a state of consciously letting go of the constraints imposed by a map and all the regimented philosophy that goes with it. Temporarily at least, follow your nose and trust your instincts.

Feel the freedom of discovering unknown territory, even (especially!) if it is in your own city. If you are walking, a good pair of shoes (or, if you are driving, a full tank of gas) greatly adds to the comfort of the process. Follow the motto "Built for comfort, not for speed."

So, the next time you travel, think twice about packing those unbearably heavy guide books in the limited space of your suitcase, and allow yourself the freedom and joy that come with going off the beaten track in a strange place. After all, unless you are rowing up the Amazon or climbing Mount Everest, there is almost always the option of catching a cab to go back home. As the old saying goes, "All roads lead to Rome."

62

Walking the World — on the Path to a Life Fully Lived

by Ward Luthi

Ward Luthi has been seeking out adventures in the great outdoors for as long as he can remember. He founded Walking The World,™ an adventure-travel program for those 50 years of age and better, in 1987. As a traveler, Luthi gives back to local communities in Central America through his nonprofit, 1stove. org, by planting trees, building schools, and providing clean cookstoves. His motto: "Get Up — Go Wild — Give Back."

Okay. You're retired or close to it. You're free from the demands of work, the kids are on their own, and you have the financial means to carry you through the years.

Now, what are you going to do with your time? Will you embrace life and dig deep into the magical adventures that are open to you in the coming years? Or will you let time slip slowly by, passing on every opportunity to reach out and grab life's great joys?

I'm going to bet that if you're reading this, you've already decided that you're not going to be a passive participant in the river of life.

The question then becomes, what is the secret to making the most of the years before you?

Since 1987, I've been designing and leading small-group walking vacations around the world for those adventurous souls 50 years of age and better. On these Walking The World trips, we've hiked in the slickrock canyons of Utah, the snow-capped mountains of Switzerland, the vineyards of Tuscany, the rain forests of Costa Rica, the towering redwood forests of California, and along the pilgrimage of St. James in Spain. And much, much more.

Over the years, these experiences in the great outdoors have slowly revealed to me the secret of living fully, a secret so powerful yet so simple that some might dismiss it as mundane and trivial. It's a secret known to many, but only a small number truly comprehend the scope of its power and the beauty of its magic. It's the key to a joyous, fulfilling, exciting, connected, mystical, awe-inspiring, and meaningful retirement.

Before I reveal what it is, though, you must know one thing: the secret holds absolutely no power if you don't use it. At the same time, you don't even need to believe that it works to gain the benefit of its powers. Simply practice the secret and the magic will be yours, guaranteed.

The secret? Pure and simple? Walking in the great outdoors.

Everything you're going to read in this essay is based on the following premise: we do best sitting around a campfire at night with family and friends, and then heading out by day to actively explore our natural world.

Nothing is better than walking out into the world and being in touch with the land beneath our feet. It helps us connect with those along the way and with all the other species that make life wondrous.

Walking is natural for us. In fact, our bodies are designed to walk. Biomechanically, it's our most efficient form of locomotion.

In our early days on Earth, our very survival required that we walk. Sitting down and waiting for life to come to us was not an option. To sit down and wait was to die. Living required that we get up and start walking. Those who explored the most were not only healthier physically, but they did better in many other ways. They found more food. They discovered more materials for building their homes and communities. They learned more about who their neighbors were. In essence, they lived more fully.

You were born to walk, and now, at this point in your life, walking can help you come back once again to a life of adventure and exploration.

Join me for a few moments as we look in on a Walking The World adventure in the American Southwest. Our destination is the Primitive Trail in Arches National Park near Moab, Utah, a seven-mile loop showcasing a variety of outstanding scenery, fabulous viewpoints, unique geology, and unforgettable photo opportunities.

After a hearty breakfast, we grab our gear, jump in the van, and make our way to the trailhead. Before we start our walk, we'll go over our plan for the day, check to ensure we all have the appropriate clothing and gear, lather on sunscreen, drink some water, and make sure our cameras are set to record the stunning beauty of the high canyon desert. We have a local guide and a Walking The World guide. One leads on the trail and one brings up the rear, partly for safety and partly so everyone benefits from the knowledge each guide brings on trail techniques and natural and cultural history.

It's late April or early May, one of the best times to visit southeast Utah. The days are warm and sunny, the skies a brilliant blue. While hiking, our goal isn't to get from point A to point B as quickly as possible, but to enjoy the spectacular scenery around us. We hike to experience, not just to observe.

I encourage everyone to see, touch, taste, feel, and smell the desert around them. To crush leaves of the desert sage between their fingers and smell the pungent aroma, to look for pine nuts in the cones of the pinyon pine, to search for the petrified tracks of the three-toed dinosaurs that used to roam the area, to breathe in the fragrant aroma of wild roses, and to be on the lookout for the vibrant blooms of the Claret Cup cactus, Indian Paintbrush, and Desert Primrose.

We stop for short informative talks about geology, desert flowers, weather, trail techniques, and the Anasazi Indians who thrived here 700 to 1,000 years ago. Hikers always seem to want to know how the Anasazi made gin from the berries of the Utah Juniper.

Normally, we hike three to four miles in the morning, then enjoy a lunch spread of fresh meats, cheeses, breads, veggies, and fruit, topped off with a variety of tempting desserts. Then, it's back on the trail for another three to four miles before returning to our hotel to freshen up prior to dinner at a local restaurant.

The most frequently asked question I get is, "Can I do this?" And in most cases, the answer is, "Yes!" At Walking The World, we believe that we all set our limits too low, that in reality we can do so much more than we ever believed possible. As such, our trips are designed to challenge you: mentally, physically, and emotionally. That being said, our guides are right there with you to lend a hand or offer moral support if there is a challenging section of trail.

Walking vacations, of any type, bring us closer together, just like sitting around a campfire at night does. And walking on paths throughout the world neatly mimics what we did in our early years on this planet. So, in essence, we've come full circle. After working at jobs that mostly kept us indoors, unconnected from our physical bodies and our physical environment, walking trips now re-create our adventurous youth. They bring us back in touch with a time when life included challenge, risk, great beauty, and intimate connection with everything and everyone around us. We faced life head-on, and there was no buffer between us and what life brought.

Whether you go on a guided walking trip with a group or head out on your own, find yourself a good pair of hiking boots and get started. Today. Automatically, the process of renewal and discovery will reconnect you with life, yourself, and the world around you.

There is no question about this. After you take that first walk, take another and another and another. Just keep walking. It doesn't matter how far or how fast you walk, just go. Walking is life. Go now. Go often.

Section

SAIL AWAY

63

Gliding Through French Wine Country

by Bill Roiter, Ed.D.

Bill Roiter, Ed.D., is a psychologist, executive coach, businessman, author, and consultant to people as they move beyond work. He is sort of retired and enjoying it. Roiter's book, *Beyond Work: How Accomplished People Retire Successfully* (Wiley, 2008), won the bookstore owners' and librarians' Axiom Gold Medal as the best retirement book of 2009. Also, he is a clinical instructor at Harvard Medical School and a consultant to many organizations, including those in the financial, higher education, life sciences, retail, health care, and not-for-profit sectors, as well as other business areas.

What would you think of a four-room, upscale hotel run by a great staff, where you sit and watch the Burgundy region of France slide by? My wife Jane and I just stayed there, and we think it's a great way to enjoy the benefits of retirement. However, unlike a B&B, this peaceful place includes three excellent meals a day as well as many snacks, hors d'oeuvres, and all the best wines and liquor you could imagine, plus fun, guided excursions. Welcome to the Orient-Express's *Hirondelle*, one of France's many guest barges that cruise the canal systems crisscrossing the countryside. Construction of the first large canals began in 1765 during the reign of Louis XVI. Poor King Louis never really had time to enjoy the canals, as he was beheaded in 1793.

I can tell you that this seven-day cruise far exceeded our already high expectations. Retirement is the best time to spend a week on a French barge. It offers a good lesson in the art of fun and relaxation.

So here is how we landed aboard our barge:

My wife researched and organized the trip. Then, we and another couple paid our not inexpensive but all-inclusive fare. Over drinks one night, we all agreed that the cost was competitive with a good resort, when you factor in all the extras for meals and drinks, tours, fees, and tips. We talked a lot over drinks.

First, on Sunday afternoon the four of us got to Paris, where a friendly driver showed up in his comfortable eight-passenger van to pick us up, along with two other couples we did not know. Three hours later, we arrived at a construction site in the town of Besançon. We were tired and hungry and somewhat grumpy and the chain-link fence and broken concrete did not humor us. But then the van doors opened, and two bright and smiling people greeted us like old friends they hadn't seen in years.

Sarah, our wonderful guide, and Cedric, our excellent captain, helped us through the construction rubble and led us to the gleaming 128- by 17-foot barge, where we were greeted with food and flutes of Champagne by three more smiling crew members who welcomed us on board. (Note: The Champagne, all the wines, and all the food we had were superb, so I won't waste adjectives mooning over them.)

Within five minutes we were having fun and relaxing — in a big and luxurious way. This isn't Trump-hotel extravagance; it's more like seaside-cottage splendor with a group of wonderful passengers and crew. This included Cedric's strong and quiet mate, Ben, who did all of our heavy lifting.

With the encouragement of our guide, Sarah, we all got to know each other — "Where are you from?" "What do you do?" — and then off we went to unpack and have our first glorious dinner. Did I mention that we had our own Chef Joe, and Nicola, his wife, who managed us on board? "Bill," she would ask me, "would you like another Jack Daniels?"

When we finished dinner the first night, we couldn't imagine eating another thing. Yet, the next morning we all woke feeling comfortable and hungry, which was fortunate given the expansive breakfast awaiting us. Each day at 8:00 a.m., the barge left our canal dock and headed out so we could enjoy the countryside passing by, with fields of corn, sunflowers, and grazing cows interspersed with very French homesteads bursting with flowers. We then cruised until about one or two in the afternoon. For the most part, we sat on the deck watching and reading and greeting the people walking or biking past on the old towpath. Occasionally, some of us would disembark and walk or bike ahead to meet the barge at the next lock or two.

These old locks raise or lower the barges to accommodate the changes in the canal water levels. The stone-and-steel locks are two feet wider and one to two feet longer than our barge. Cedric and Ben are experts at stuffing this big boat into these small boxes. Then the lock is either flooded to raise us up or drained to lower us. Most of the working locks were built in the early 1800s, and sailing through them is great fun.

After lunch, we would all leave the barge and climb into Sarah's big van for an afternoon excursion. There were tours of the vineyards of Burgundy, Chateau wine-tastings, the beautiful 500-year-old Hôtel-Dieu (Hospital for the Poor) in Beaune, and busy market days in small villages, where we would wander and Sarah would buy fresh produce, meats, breads, and sweets for Chef Joe to turn into more sumptuous meals. Then it was back to our barge for more talk, more wine, and more food. We got used to this life very quickly, and we never tired of it.

As happens with most things that are too good to last, it was suddenly Saturday and time to leave for Paris. As the old travelogues would say in closing, "We bid adieu to our new friends with hopes of seeing them all again."

If you have the itch to cruise on a canal barge, I suggest that you bring:

- some people you enjoy. Four couples can book the entire barge. If you can't round up some others, then you should bring along a willingness to meet like-minded folks and get to know them. We were fortunate to share our trip with people we got along with so well.

- a desire to do little or nothing at all for half of each day. If you can't sit still, bring books, games, your laptop, etc., to distract you while your new friends delight in the view of France as it slides by.

- an enjoyment of food and wine; it supplies half of the fun of the journey. If you have food restrictions, you can inform the crew when you complete your written profile prior to the trip. I swear our crew memorized the profile of each person.

- a sense of fun. Our guide, Sarah, did a great job of entertaining us during the excursions. You can savor your adventures or not; it's up to you. Do you notice how possessive I'm sounding about our barge and our crew? It's part of the barge experience.

- a camera, casual clothes, and whatever else will add to your happiness. Try to pack light. Of course, we did not!

For those of you interested in the *Hirondelle* barge cruise, you can check out their Web site at www. hirondellebarge.com.

64

Sailing into Retirement

by Edwin Jacks

Edwin Jacks worked as a computer engineer and engineering manager at Intel Corporation for 26 years, while his wife, Ann, put her business career on hold to rear their four children. She served nine years as a school-board director while continuing to volunteer in the schools. They have also run a ski bus for middle and high school kids, served on the Mt. Hood Ski Patrol, played adult soccer, coached sports teams, and now root for the Oregon Ducks, Beavers, and Portland State Vikings. They live in the greater Portland, Oregon, area. During the boating off-season, they swim, road bike, mountain bike, camp, volunteer, and ballroom dance. Ann is an avid gardener, and Ed is her assistant.

My love of boating began when I was young, cruising on the Great Lakes in my father's cabin cruiser. Many years later, I retired so that I would have the opportunity to be outdoors instead of inside on beautiful days, and to find time for other passions. Most of all, I wanted to sail. But when I first retired, I had questions about sailing. I wondered:

How would I handle seasickness? Would I like moving at the slow speed of a sailboat? Would my wife, Ann, find enjoyment being on a boat? To prepare, I crewed on a schooner in the Caribbean for five weeks, where I survived seasickness and learned a lot of lessons about how *not* to maintain a boat. I found out about the crewing opportunity via one of the Web sites that help captains find a crew. My wife and I took sailing lessons, then signed on as crew members for a young couple, taking their boat from San Diego to Mexico. That was when Ann uttered the fateful words, "We should buy a sailboat." Before she could change her mind, we were out looking at boats.

We purchased a 38-foot sailboat one year after my retirement. It is the first boat that either of us has ever owned. We realized that we lacked the experience to make a difficult voyage right off, so we decided that it would be best for us to sail to the Bahamas and the Caribbean. This bicoastal plan has worked well, with great sailing during the wet winters of Oregon and great land living during the wonderful northwest summers.

I love the idea of being propelled by the wind and facing the technical challenges of sailing a boat. My wife and I have spent many hours in classes and boating to learn the skills appropriate to sailing and the cruising lifestyle. I advise people interested in sailing to look into lessons from professional instructors; for example, the American Sailing Association (ASA) is a good resource. The United States Power Squadron (USPS) and the ASA provide classes in navigation and "rules of the road." The ASA also offers hands-on sailing instruction for everything from the basics through advanced offshore sailing. Be sure that your partner also learns and is your sailing buddy. Not only may it save your life, but it will also strengthen your relationship.

I have met two couples who did not take all the steps we did before boat ownership. Both have sold their boats and gone back to land life. One couple was unprepared for the fear that the wife experienced being away from land. The other couple purchased a racing trimaran unsuited to cruising. We barely escaped the same fate for another reason: after our first three months of boat ownership, we had not done anything except spend money and move the boat north from Miami to a boat yard in Georgia. At the time, my wife felt the financial obligations were outweighing the enjoyment of boat ownership. But I told her that sailing was my dream, and fortunately she gave it another try the following fall and fell in love with the Bahamas. I became a sort of hero to my friends, who were all trying to convince their wives to go sailing.

People have the impression that we are always sailing, but that is not the case. We sail to destinations such as Georgetown, the Bahamas, or the Grenadines in the Caribbean Windward Island group and stay for weeks, even months, snorkeling, fishing, hiking, getting to know the people, and exploring the area. But most of our trips are measured in hours rather than days. We typically do overnight sails only a few nights per season, but we do day trips between the islands frequently.

So, how long will we keep cruising? We're not sure, but we keep finding new places to go in the Caribbean, and we're now even thinking about sailing to Europe and the southwest Pacific. Or we might shorten up our season and do some skiing one winter. One thing's for sure: we still enjoy the lifestyle and making our friends in the northwest envious by complaining about the heat and sun, while they're enduring gray skies and rain.

65

Sailing the Mystery: My Journey into the Unknown

by Ed Merck

Ed Merck spent 30 rewarding years as chief financial officer and a music faculty member at several prestigious universities and colleges. Subsequently, assuming the role of business entrepreneur, he codeveloped Future Perfect, the premier computer-based strategic/financial planning model used in higher education today. In recent years, Merck has gravitated towards pursuits of the heart — writing, making music, teaching yoga, sailing the East Coast of America, and offering workshops in "Conscious Aging." His book, *Sailing the Mystery: My Journey into Life's Remaining Chapters*, was released in February 2013. He currently resides in Rhode Island and can be reached at www.sailingthemystery.com.

I n what seemed like an instant, I retired from full-time work, my marriage unraveled, and my son went off to college. Yikes, I didn't know who I was anymore. On a good day, my identity as a father, spouse, and business entrepreneur seemed outdated and irrelevant. It felt like everything had been taken away — or worse, that I had bet my life on what I thought was a good hand, and lost.

This much was clear: I was done living out our culture's stock formulas for fulfillment. Instead, I felt a determination within to discover my own version of what it meant to embrace the final chapters with vitality and purpose. I could hear the Universe speaking to me: *Feel the exhilaration that comes from embracing the implicit danger of the unknown.* Yet I had only the slightest awareness of how to construct such a reality.

I was 62 then — my time to kick back and reap the hard-earned rewards of a life well lived, or at least that's what society had wanted me to believe. Instead, I felt caught in the painful swirl of a life defined by ambiguity, without a ready identity to fall back on.

What to do? Left to my own devices, I would likely continue to delay important choices, feeling deceptively safe in the assumption that there was plenty of time remaining. But would I really be in good enough physical and mental shape to address some of those important dreams tomorrow — not to mention when I reached my 70s, then only eight years away?

Unexpected spine surgery that same year drove home the point of my relentless aging. Due to nerve damage from an otherwise successful operation, my walk took on a slight and —to me, at least — embarrassing limp. Was I running out of good healthy time? Was this my last chance?

Motivated by the wake-up call, I made a list of must-do intentions that, with a little work, I reduced down to two items: 1) grow more inwardly spiritual (which embraced activities such as making more music and developing a steady meditation practice), and 2) engage in more blue-water (open ocean) sailing. No surprise — the two were mutually reinforcing. I realized, even then, that living on the water held the potential to address both the concrete and the intangible, a deep connection to the ocean and a boost in consciousness.

So, I went to the sea to find myself anew, knowing that only a full immersion into the energy of the ocean would bring me home to my authentic self. Arriving at my deathbed without having at least tried out my dream of long-distance sailing was unacceptable, even if I ended up not liking it. In my view, the only failure would be not having tried.

Following the call of my newly rediscovered spirit, I sold my house, bought a boat, and set sail. Along the way there was plenty of adventure — fiery romantic trials, a deepening bond with my only son, emerging spiritual insights, the sweet love of friends, and the blaze of self-transformation. All that in pursuit of a more in-depth, engaged life, played out against the uncertain and often challenging course of my aging.

Living on my 36-foot sailing vessel, *Kairos*, round-the-clock in the middle of the Atlantic, was a uniquely profound experience for me. It flowed from my close and developing intimacy with the natural elements — a continuous meditation on merging with the power and beauty of endless sky, water, and wind. Far from the regimentation of steady work and family routine, days ran into nights ran into days, all passing silently as I allowed myself to be lulled into an exceptional state of bliss, moment by moment by moment.

Romance was truly in abundance, riding the ocean 24/7. Dolphins (such elegant beings) became my friends, offering frequent visits while I watched and applauded their joyful play. Flying fish leapt over and occasionally onto *Kairos*, and plentiful species of birds — even butterflies — flew all about me. There were magnificent sunrises, sunsets, moonrises, and moonsets; gorgeous blue, blue, and more blue from both water and sky in every direction; and an almost mystical solitude, especially alone on watch. My favorite time was deep into the night with a full moon. The intense light illuminated the breaking surf, creating a beautiful phosphorescent white skirt for *Kairos*, as I glided along gracefully on nothing but wind power.

One year after departing for my first voyage on *Kairos*, I celebrated the completion of a successful round-trip sail of the East Coast of America, something I wouldn't have believed possible only 12 months prior. I went to the sea to feel the vitality that comes from living life on the edge; to feel life's wildness coursing through my veins. I also went to the sea to engage risk; to free myself from the safe psychological box I had lived in. The result is a new me, one who often moves gracefully into the unknown, while diving into the free fall of life without clinging to the familiar.

That year of concentrated, often dangerous adventure out on the water helped me to feel more alive. And by strengthening my inner landscape, I am now better

able to surrender into the natural way of things —
something I learned by continually watching the waves
form, and then dissolve back again into the ocean. Of
course I'm still a student, and hopefully a humble one,
with oh so much more to learn.

I had no idea how this year of intense transition
and personal growth would evolve when I set sail.
At times it was scary — life-threateningly scary —
especially after my realization that there wasn't even
a destination to be had, merely a process. I sailed
into the mystery, only to discover that life is not about
resolution. We just keep adding capacity to engage
more of the mystery. And that is the miracle.

About the Editor

Mark Evan Chimsky is the head of Mark Chimsky Editorial Services Unlimited, an editorial consulting business based in Portland, Maine. For nearly six years, he was the editor in chief of the book division of Sellers Publishing, an independent publishing company in South Portland, Maine. Previously he was executive editor and editorial director of Harper San Francisco and headed the paperback divisions at Little, Brown and Macmillan. In addition, he was on the faculty of New York University's Center for Publishing, and for three years he served as the director of the book section of NYU's Summer Publishing Institute. He has edited a number of best-selling books, including Johnny Cash's memoir, *Cash*, and he has worked with such notable authors as Melody Beattie, Arthur Hertzberg, Beryl Bender Birch, and Robert Coles. He was also project manager on Billy Graham's *New York Times* best-selling memoir, *Just As I Am*. He conceived of the long-running series *The Best American Erotica*, which was compiled by Susie Bright, and he was the first editor to reissue the works of celebrated novelist Dawn Powell. His editorial achievements have been noted in *Vanity Fair*, the *Nation*, and *Publishers Weekly*. He is an award-winning poet whose poetry and essays have appeared in *JAMA* (the *Journal of the American Medical Association*), *Wild Violet*, *Three Rivers Poetry Journal*, and *Mississippi Review*. For Sellers Publishing, he developed and compiled a number of acclaimed books, including *Creating a Life You'll Love*, which won the silver in ForeWord's 2009 Book of the Year Awards (self-help category) and *65 Things to Do When You Retire*, which the *Wall Street Journal* called "[one of] the year's best guides to later life." In addition to helping authors develop marketable proposals and manuscripts, Mark teaches in the Writing, Literature, and Publishing Department at Emerson College in Boston.

Credits

"Retirement Travel Will Renew Your Sense of Excitement About the World"©
2013 Ernie J. Zelinski; "Travel-Planning Logistics" © 2013 Mahara Sinclaire;
"Senior Travel Deals" © 2013 Ed Perkins; "Rewire® Your Travel" © 2013
Rewire®; "The Art of Authentic Travel" © 2013 Doris Gallan; "Solo Travel"
© 2013 Janice Waugh; "Is Traveling Really the Retirement Dream?" ©
2013 Jim Yih; "Improve Your Retirement Travel with Internet Tools and
Social Media" © 2013 Ron Mercier; "Leverging Excess Good Credit" ©
2013 Rick Ingersoll; "Shopping Across Borders for Medical Care" © 2013
Traveling4Health; "Traveling Sin" © 2013 Rick Kimball; "Getting the Most
from a Private Tour Guide" © 2013 www.ispyrome.com; "The Let's Sell-Our-
House-and-See-the-World Retirement Plan" © 2013 Lynne Martin; "What
Retirees Can Learn from Career Breakers" © 2013 JJJ Enterprises, LLC;
"Gap Years Are Wasted on the Young" © 2013 Jo Carroll; "Start with Your 'A'
List" © 2013 Michael Jeans; "Unconventional Travelers" © 2013 E & J Howle;
"Change Through Travel — It's Easier Than You Think" © 2013 Christine T.
Mackay; "We Traveled the World for Two Years, Enhancing Our Lives with
More Adventure and Romance" © 2013 Wayne Dunlap (Plan Your Escape);
"Never a Still Moment" © 2013 Leyla Alyanak; "Pick the Right Places, and
Traveling Is Not Expensive" © 2013 Tim Leffel; "Just a Backpack and a
Rollie" © 2013 JustaBackpackandaRollie; "Glamping for Retirees" © 2013
Abby Jeffords; "Look Local for Great Times" © 2013 Mike Bonacorsi; "A
Great Gal-loping Getaway" © 2013 Jane Cassie; "Voluntourism" © 2013 Jim
T. Miller; "Earthwatch Adventures" © 2013 Warren Stortroen; "Clem" © 2013
Ruth Clemmer; "Somewhere in the World with Peter and Hinda" © 2013
Peter and Hinda Schnurman; "Change Your World! Volunteer!" © 2013 Billy
and Akaisha Kaderli; "Important Conversations with Your Partner about
Retirement Travel" © 2013 Dorian Mintzer; "Maybe I Protest Too Much.
Maybe Not." © 2013 Samuel Jay Keyser; "Travel to Rediscover Your Family
Heritage" © 2013 Dave Bernard; "Retirement Travel — a Family Affair" ©
2013 Dan Austin; "Enrich Your Life" © 2013 Sam Dalton; "Travels with [Insert
Your Pet's Name Here]" © 2013 Chris Kingsley; "A Cartoon" © 2013 Mort
Gerberg; "Writing Workshops" © 2013 Elizabeth Berg; "Wine Tourism" © 2013
George M. Taber; "A Magical Cooking Experience on the Amalfi Coast" ©
2013 Karen Herbst; "Ranch Vacations" © 2013 Gene Kilgore; "Transformative
Tanzania 'Inventure'" © 2013 Margaret L. Newhouse; "A Quest for Wonder"
© 2013 Richard Bangs; "A Gift" © 2013 Maeona (Mae) Mendelson; "Seven